THE REVOLUTIONARY YEAR

THE

REVOLUTIONARY

YEAR

Recapturing the Meaning of the Church Year

by JAY C. ROCHELLE

FORTRESS PRESS

Philadelphia

Library of Congress Catalog Card Number 72–87065

ISBN 0–8006–0129–7

3471H72   Printed in the United States of America   1–129

CONTENTS

INTRODUCTION

Liturgy, like theology, tries to relate the word of God and the experience of man. When it does this it is alive. But often it does not do this, and then it seems remote, distant, unrelated to the world of man and his experience. Particularly in Western Christianity individual religious experience, rather than being supported by and correlated with history, has frequently been negated. The church has seemed more interested in the superimposition of a (historic) religious experience than in the investigation and clarification of individual experience. As a result, lines have been artificially drawn between "sacred" and "secular" history and experience. It is assumed that all of history and experience is not sacred, or religious; the biblical records and the church's language give the sacred history and experience. The church *tells* people what religious experience is, rather than giving people a model by which to interpret their own sacred history. A line is drawn between the "teaching church," which is assumed to be the repository of religious experience, and the laity who remain in the dark. When this antithesis is seen as false, people simply drop out rather than fight the religious imperialism they feel. Unable to appropriate the intellectual content of the faith in which they have been brought up, and told that their own experience is not "religious" and has little or no connection with the sacred history, they join the legions of self-imposed exiles from the church.

One of the basic theses of this book is that if the church is to survive, its liturgy or worship cannot limit itself to a historical and rational presentation. Contemporary experience, particularly the existential/mystical dimensions of that experience, must find a place within the church's worship.

We will argue in this book (building on the central thesis of *Create and Celebrate**) that the church's liturgical year offers a model for the organization of individual religious experience into a meaningful whole. Correctly understood and used the liturgical year can be a bridge between our historical/rational background and the existential/mystical side of our experience.

The problem of the liturgical year is very simple. It *is* historical, and we are living in an age when historical conditioning is suspect. The primary mode of experience today has shifted from historical reflection to the existential moment's meaning. This leaves two options for the church: (1) it must give up the church year because of the historical conditioning of its major festivals, recognizing that history as reflection on the past is not of primary importance to most people today; or (2) it must demonstrate the existential dimensions of the major festivals to show the connection between sacred history (reflection on the past) and existential "history" (reflection on personal experience). This book uses the second option.

The first reason for making this choice is our conviction that, to help people retrieve a historical dimension to life, the church must offer "hooks" or "links" by which to organize individual experience into a meaningful body. We are at a crucial time in our culture. The culture is oppressively Apollonian in flavor and content; the subculture is almost wholly Dionysian. Christianity's original identification was primarily with the Dionysian culture, the culture of spontaneity and freedom, but it has lost that impetus. There is a need for balance because both emphases in the extreme lead to madness. The church has the opportunity to bridge creatively the gap between the two cultures by assisting people in filling the experience of the existential moment with a historic dimension.

The second reason for sticking with the liturgical year is that the great festivals do correlate to experience. The problem is, of

---

* Jay C. Rochelle, *Create and Celebrate* (Philadelphia: Fortress Press, 1971).

course, that we cannot force individual religious experience into a pattern such as the church year. People will continue to feel like "Lent" in the midst of "Advent" and there is nothing we can do about that. But if we wish to remain in the liturgical tradition, then we have got to penetrate the reality below the history, and at least *offer* the system. If we examine the historical shell of the church year, we find that it does correlate to an ongoing process which people undergo throughout their lives: the organization of (religious) experience into a meaningful whole. There are the up times, there are the down times; there are times of openness followed by periods of insularity and introspection; there are experiences of death and resurrection. There are periods for investigating one's response to the world. There are periods for the pure celebration of the affirmation at the base of life. What we do within the revolutionary year is to organize these into a meaningful whole, which assists people to organize their own experience. Man is a creature of times, both *chronos* and *kairos*. The *kairos*-event is an event in which transcendence is comprehended as the depth within experience. The church's main emphasis is on *kairos* and this is where it should stay, but we have to recognize that our culture does not recognize that time can be significant, because it is wholly oriented to *chronos*. The Protestant church has frequently viewed Christian liturgy exclusively on a *chronos*-level. Where a church emphasizes only *chronos* (the past events of faith in history) it may relate to people where they are, but it will fail to relate anything significant to their experience which can add the sacred dimension to life, or amplify it, because it is relating on the level of their meaninglessness.

The distinction between *chronos* and *kairos* works liturgically in the distinction between traditional worship and contemporary celebration. Celebration is not merely the updating of liturgical forms; it is not the performance of an occasional jazz mass. Traditional worship is the honor given a "sacred" object outside the normal range of human experience; it has an ethereal, almost unreal, quality to it. It is disconnected from present experience. Contemporary celebration is the awareness of the sacred dimension within the *ordinary*. Its model is the Eucharist understood as sanctification of the commonplace, the presence of God in the everyday.

The liturgy stands as the doorway between the tradition of the faith and the experience of individual faith. It is this position which raises liturgy, the *form* of which may remain neutral, out of the arena of worthless questions and gives it crucial importance. Liturgy is a demonstration of the Christian life-style and faith, and as such we must continually ask the question, "What is being demonstrated here?" If our liturgical life demonstrates only the historical continuum of Christianity, then it falls short of a presentation of total faith. If our liturgical life demonstrates only the level of human relationships implied in the gospel, then we have failed to give the depth necessary to underwrite experience as *religious*.

The function of the revolutionary year is to present the panorama of the historic faith of Christianity in such a way that it matches the inner experience of the participant in the liturgical process. That the revolutionary year can do this poorly or well is obvious, and it is in large part dependent on how well we understand this function, how deep the content, experience, and faith of the managers of the liturgical forms are, and how committed we are to giving a balanced picture of the faith for the lives we work and worship with. This little book is an attempt to take seriously individual religious experience *and* the collective historical tradition of the revolutionary year and to achieve a synthesis which damages neither.

I have called the church year the revolutionary year for a reason, and the reason has nothing to do with gimmickry or literary device. The reason is that, properly understood from both an emotional and an intellectual perspective, the church year assists us to undergo personal and communal revolution each year we celebrate it. It is a tool for the organization of religious experience, both the collective historical experience of the church, and the individual experience of faith.

SOME NOTES ON THE LITURGIES FOR THE REVOLUTIONARY YEAR

Some notes are necessary in conjunction with these liturgies. The first thing to be noticed about them is that they are skeletal patterns. Words are kept to a minimum. The outline of the historic liturgy is within each of these services. The demonstration of the Christian life-style which the liturgy proclaims to the community and the world is retained, in fact enhanced, by the skeletal nature of these liturgies.

The second thing to be noticed is that they are altered for each of the seasons of the revolutionary year, and that there is a special liturgy for the celebration of saints' days, too. The modifications in these services from season to season look slight, but when you consider the fact that they are terribly reduced in verbal content, the changes made are *enough* to shift the emphasis of the worshipping community to the seasonal input.

The third thing to be noticed is that the dramatization of additional input for the shape of each season is up to the individual community. The choice of songs, for example, could be different from season to season depending on how large a selection you have. The use of different aids for dramatization, such as incense and the setting of mood, is up to the community. The one warning we would throw in is that you want, at all costs, to avoid the "gimmicky" and the sensational. The liturgical pattern has enough drama and emotion on its own to stand without a lot of additional gimmicks.

The fourth thing to notice about these liturgies is that they depend on two human factors that are highly important:

(1) It is fully expected that *each person will participate* to the fullest in this liturgical pattern. These are not liturgies as spectator sports. They will lose their effectiveness if they are celebrated as such. They take seriously the concept of liturgy as "the work of the people." For this reason, it is advisable to work your way into them either through explanatory periods about their use, or through experiential designs that demonstrate, one by one, the inner meaning of each of the parts of worship. This participation is further underwritten by the prior understanding that *everything*

in the liturgical pattern, with the exception of the contemporary word (and even this can be excepted occasionally) and the Eucharistic Canon, is to be done by members of the celebrating community. We mean this note to be taken seriously: *everything* else is to be done by members of the community, including the baking of the bread (or its purchase) and the making of the wine (or its purchase). As time goes on, a songbook used in conjunction with these liturgies ought also to be written by the community, or its individual members. These liturgies are meant as expressions of the life of an individual community of Christ, which means that the needs and desires and joys of that community must be taken into account. The form admits of such individual input while retaining enough historic form to incorporate new people as the community grows.

(2) The participatory structure of these services demands a different understanding of the role of pastor in worship. The pastor must become the liturgical president again, the "master of ceremonies" who senses the drift of the liturgy and eases it from one portion to another. (See the discussion in chapter 9 on the behavioral style of the liturgical president.)

It is useful for the liturgical president to compile his own celebration book which would include additional materials in the form of a collection of eucharistic prayers. Although a skilled president should be able to utilize the materials from an evening's celebration to spin his own prayer for the night, nevertheless a collection of them offers wider variety. Similarly, the celebration books ought to contain a larger collection of Affirmations (creeds) than is given here (one for each liturgy). The celebration book of the Community of the Spirit, of which the author is currently liturgical president, contains at present twenty-two different creeds. The creed used during a celebration is chosen by an individual during the celebration.

(Another note: the Celebration Book of the Community of the Spirit, in addition to the liturgies and the additional Affirmations, contains a songbook section divided into six different categories:

Getting Started—songs useful for opening the liturgy

Getting the Word—songs useful to tune people in to a consideration of the word

Songs of Peace and Freedom—used anytime during a celebration

Sharing the Meal—communion songs

Breaking Out—songs for the close of service

Special Times—songs especially for Christ-mass, Easter, etc.
The celebration book currently contains over 100 songs.)

The fifth thing to notice about these liturgies is in the nature of a thought for consideration. These liturgies, it is obvious, will not work in the ordinary milieu of a Sunday congregational worship setting. These are meant for small-group celebration. Our experience has led us to believe that the maximum number of people with whom they can be celebrated and still retain their spontaneity, intimacy, and total participation is about thirty-five. Twenty-five to thirty seems to be the optimum range.

The sixth note is again a thought for consideration. We have found it helpful to print a two-page brochure entitled "Celebration at The Community of the Spirit," which was brainstormed by the core group of the community. This brochure is used when new people come, to assist them in seeing the correlation with the historic liturgical pattern and to make them feel part of the celebration before it begins. A member of the community usually sits with such a person and goes through the brochure before the celebration begins.

Break on through
to the other side
Beyond good and evil
where the fat chance
and the sure thing
both dissolve in mist.

Break on through
to the other side
where life is celebration
and celebration is life
where yes and no
unite in YES.

Break on through
to the other side
where mind and body
their parts unite
and the whole
greater than the sum.

1

FAITH AND MEMORY

Liturgy is an attitude, an approach to life, a demonstration of the way of life for committed Christians. Whatever else it may be, it is for committed Christians. The moment we discover that commitment is what liturgy requires, we have entered the domain of faith. Faith does not operate without commitment; commitment is an outgrowth of faith. They belong together. And so it is not only natural but almost necessary to look at faith before we look at liturgy, even so highly structured a form of liturgy as the church year.

Someone has characterized our age as an age of "faithless content and contentless faith." The church seems to fail today because of a lack of *authority* in its life. If the trumpet gives an uncertain sound, nobody is going to get ready for battle. We have too many "trumpets" and the "sounds" conflict in a cacophony. Authority is lacking. Yet the church's only authority is in its faith, ultimately; in the conviction that it conveys, in some way, truth to man. This is what keeps it alive as an institution. This is what keeps it alive as a community.

Faith has two sides: as an objective phenomenon, it is the record of religious experience. As a subjective phenomenon, it is the apprehension of the reality of God within the individual's life that gives him root and meaning; it is a relationship. It can be investigated on both of these levels.

1

The external body of statements about Christianity is the "faith which is believed." It is the objective statement of a community of Christians. It has historical roots; it stretches across time to the ancient church, to the apostolic age and the fathers of the Christian revolution; it encompasses, in some measure, the great upheavals which split the church into two halves (East and West) and the later upheaval which split the Western church into further camps (Protestant and Roman Catholic). It frequently incorporates the ancient creeds of the church: the Apostles' and the Nicene, with perhaps the Athanasian Creed thrown in for good measure. Yet at the same time it is being consistently and continuously rewritten to speak the word to *now*. The church holds such a body of faith out to members and nonmembers alike not as a taunt or a piece of bait, but as a corporate witness which it calls men to examine, to test, to measure against the reality of their own experience. The creeds, for example, are less statements of doctrinal content and more doxologies: hymns of praise to God couched in the language which first captured men's experience of God. As people enter this living stream, they find that they are capable of identifying themselves with people who lived one hundred, five hundred, a thousand years ago. The experience is, after all, the same; it is just in different words and linguistic models. They find that they are engrafted into the "red thread of tradition," as Luther called it, the faith of the church which stretches back in time to the first revolution: the cross and Resurrection of Christ. The reason it is possible to identify with this tradition is that the tradition is an embodiment of the collective experience of truth by a great number of people. Furthermore, the verbal handles on that truth remain relatively consistent, as signposts on the road of experience. For the experienced Christian, they perform a function like that of shorthand. The Christian who penetrates the reality of God understands that his verbal proclamation is wholly secondary to the experience, but simultaneously he realizes that it is necessary to assist others in organizing their own experience. The church preserves a body of tradition from the past, not because it is hung up on the past (although that seems to be the impression that is given), but because the past experience relates to the contemporary experience of God. The tradition serves as a guide.

The church uses liturgy as a tool to preserve, remember, and demonstrate the experience which is collected in this so-called received faith. This is one of the central functions of liturgy. Liturgy is a means of engrafting people into a body, the Body of Christ, and part of that Body is the body of faith which we have received from the past. Unless we are complete fools, we pay attention to that body of faith and use our minds to distinguish what is real from that which is unrealistic, that which is identifiable within our own life-experience from that which is not. But we don't jettison the whole thing simply because we have difficulty identifying with it; that is anarchistic.

But there is another side to the matter. There is not only a faith which is believed (tradition), there is a faith by which one lives. There is subjectivity as well as objectivity. Faith and belief are different. Belief is only a mental catalog of the intellectual handles you put on faith; faith is the whole relationship, an attitude of wonder and trust and joy, based on the realization that the reality at the center of life is friendly and not hostile (God is love). Faith is a word of relationship and not of intellectual content. Which is not to say that it cannot be expressed intellectually; otherwise it would be totally incommunicable.

For classical theologians, faith had three parts: *notitia, assensus* and *fiducia. Notitia* is the knowledge that there is something which a man can get hold of to give meaning to his life, and furthermore it is the direction to the place where he can find it. The Protestant church has emphasized the Bible as the place where it can be found. The church catholic has pointed to the community as the bearer of the meaning. *Notitia* points to the assumption that reality can be found, that there is a core to life which can be penetrated, that man can rest in God. *Notitia* is the observation that there is something and not nothing which undergirds the universe and the life of the individual. *Notitia* is, existentially, the recognition that man is something but that he is not everything. It is a part of faith.

Assensus refers to belief, to the accumulation of a number of intellectual handles, by which the information given the senses in the experience of *notitia* may be gathered and organized rationally. *Assensus* occurs on the intellectual level, and it produces a content which it is possible to communicate in a rational way so that others can understand it mentally. Older Protestant theology so overemphasized *assensus* that it appeared as if this was the primary meaning of faith. What we are saying here is that it is only a *part* of a total concept of faith. It is not the whole thing, and the moment it is made the whole thing the sense of wonder and joy which occurs on the primary level of experience begins to shrivel and die. *Assensus* is like taking a rose, stripping its petals, stamen and pistel and stem apart, then putting it on a table and proudly declaring "Here is a rose!" But the rose is gone, analyzed into oblivion. The overemphasis on *assensus* within the Protestant tradition has had much the same effect on the experience of God.

Fiducia is the childlike trust placed in the experience of God. It is the relationship which is entered with God on the basis of the experience that he is love. Put in other terms, it is trust that the universe is cosmos and not chaos, in the primitive sense that the universe may be trusted rather than feared. This trust is a gift; it cannot be produced externally. It is an inner comprehension that occurs in the life of the individual.

The search for a synthesis between the objective tradition and the subjective experience is maddening. Obviously we can err in both directions. If subjectivity is overemphasized, we wind up with a community of people who judge the nature of God on the basis of their own feeling-state at a given time (which is the opposite of the meaning of grace: a free gift not dependent on the emotionalism of the recipient—see Eph. 2:8 f.). If objectivity is overemphasized, the risk is run that there will be no correlation between the communication of the church and the experience of the individual to whom it supposedly speaks.

It is the function of the church to assist the individual in seeing the correlation between his own faith (*notitia, assensus,* and *fiducia* all together) and the faith which is the body of tradition in the church. All of the intimations of the divine which men feel in themselves, in their relationships, in their apprehension of nature, can be bound up by the community and given meaning. But the church no longer fulfills its function when it does not take seriously the religious experience of the individual and tries to program him to fit ready-made molds of religious experience from the past.

The liturgical year—or revolutionary year as we prefer to call it— is one instrument in the church's possession that has the potential of bringing together the religious experience of the individual and the religious experience from the past. If we take the time to examine the liturgical year to see what it contains, some pleasant surprises are in store. For one thing, the ancient fathers of the revolution who put most of the church year together were no fools. They consciously used their skills to try to re-create history, both the past history of the faith and the "history" of the individual's experience, so that the community of faith would have a tool for raising consciousness which was worth keeping a few years. They would probably be surprised that their tool has lasted so long. Not all the materials they created or chose communicate that well anymore. This is understandable because we don't use the same language now as they did in the third, fourth, or fifth centuries. Their biblical pericopes need work because they don't have the inner consistency at some of the "less crucial" periods of the year that they have at Christmas and Easter, for example. But basically the fathers of the revolution impress us as an incredibly bright and experienced group of people. They gave us a tool which, if worked with properly, can still sensitize people to the presence of God in their own history and convey the inner meaning of the Christ-event.

This is why the church year is the revolutionary year; it does sensitize us to the past of the faith, shows us how to interpret the past of our own lives, and offers us models for projection into a radically redesigned future viewed from the perspective of the kingdom of God. The church year is the revolutionary year because it calls us, collectively and individually, to undergo a process of constant repentance (turning about; changing our minds; altering our life-style; remolding our consciousness—to cite some ideas of what repentance means). Out of repentance comes revolution, that kind of creative break from the past which is at the same time a new affiliation with the past. God is the author of the experience of deepening enlightenment in an individual's life, and enlightenment always involves saying yes and no to aspects of the past. The revolutionary year is a tool for consistently re-creating the matrix within which breaks from the past are possible which deepen our existence by planting it more firmly in God's reality.

The revolutionary year matches the depth of human experience. By virtue of its deep catholicity, it is simultaneously "protestant" in the true sense that it continually protests against static faith and forces us into the dynamic mold of pilgrimage: "We have here no abiding city." The very fact that it is marked by change helps us to see that change is the only permanent thing about life, and that the clinging, grasping mentality of many moderns is ridiculous in the extreme. The mood of pilgrimage in the Christian tradition is nothing other than the recognition that we cannot *grasp* God, possess him, hold him tight, but must move through life with him.

The individual pilgrim faith demands a pilgrim community, but the pilgrim community needs stakes, marking poles by which to guide its pilgrimage lest it fall off either side of the path into dogmatism or anarchy. The revolutionary year is a large part of the path the pilgrim community trods, and its great festivals are the stakes.

Christianity needs radical models for celebration if it is to survive and revive the church of our age. We think it can survive. We think that one of the models for celebration whose radical nature can be unearthed is the church's year. This book deals with the spirit and identity of each season of the revolutionary year as a whole; specifics are not dealt with here; literally hundreds of books can be consulted for the specifics of the seasons. The spirit is what is important, because it is the spirit which indicates the type of individual religious experience that each season relates to. Bearing in mind the central thesis, that the revolutionary year is a model for organizing religious experience into a meaningful *Gestalt* by which to live, we move into the seasons that make up this year.

BACK TO THE ROOTS

So now it has come to this;
So we've come to this point—
It may have been reached before—
Where the sickness of the times
And the stench of hollow words
Demand the name of Christ
be hidden within the folds of the world.
Underground once more.

Strangely we can name him in our hearts
But must be careful about his mention out loud
Not because of those who reject.him
But because of those who say
They believe in him
Yet so distort his meaning
And confuse his presence
That it seems ironically
better not to name him at all
except in celebration
    where the community
    can receive him anew
    with true meaning
    and boundless power.
Underground once more.

2

RADICAL CHRIST-MASS:

THANKS FOR HISTORY!

The Christ-mass message is so blurred by sentimental overtones that it is increasingly hard to penetrate its core. Tom Lehrer's immortal tribute, "Angels we have heard on high, telling us 'Go out and buy'" really rings true.

Now I have no need or desire to devalue holiday traditions of festivity and food and family gatherings. In fact, in our highly mobile, technological society the need to gather people into a primary communal matrix (the family) to celebrate the gifts of love they bear one another is probably greater than in the past. The hook in this is that such traditions are directly related to what already exists; no amount of tradition laid as a veneer on an un-loving situation can possibly create the love that doesn't exist in the first place. Tradition is an outgrowth of reality, not a substitute for it.

We need, if we can, to approach Christ-mass with a threefold vision in which *past* and *future* merge into *present*.

The *past* vision is the celebration of the birth of a child, of obscure historical interest to many people, and certainly to those among whom he was born. He was called "Jesus" or "Jehoshua," a Hebrew word meaning "saviour," a name rich in tradition as the name of Moses' successor as leader of Israel. This is the memory which Christianity keeps alive by celebrating Christ-mass.

9

But the past vision is also connected with the "memory" that, at a particular time and place, the reality of God was evident in, with, and under the world of man, not as a "supernatural" intrusion to reality but as the real at the base of reality, the divine within the profane, the sacred in the midst of the secular, the eternal in the center of the temporal. Christ-mass celebrates that God was evident among men. It is the confirmation of man's discovery that he can love and be loved because he is *accepted* at the core of his being. But it is not only confirmation; it is also paradigm, model of the truth of God's presence. The historical figure of Jesus has a continuing relevance for the church and the world because of this paradigmatic character of Christ-mass.

Christ-mass celebrates the en-flesh-ment (incarnation) of God, which to our knowledge hasn't been rescinded, but which we have for the most part failed to take seriously. Hung up as we are with our puritan background, we have trouble celebrating the joys of the flesh as being within the purview of God's reality and design for man. Hence, one wonders how often and with what success we are able to celebrate Christ-mass at all, since we bypass its crucial message (God coming in the *body* of mankind) and stick with words and songs, only occasionally touching close with *things* (bread and wine and candles and incense). Christ-mass announces the materiality of the spiritual; the spirituality of the material. The liturgy of the church is a sign of this materiality, but we so often shun it.

Christ-mass also celebrates the identification of God with the lot of the poor; God comes not only in radical acceptance and in the flesh: he comes in *poor* flesh. Again, we must take seriously the poverty of God. He comes with no means available to coerce us into accepting him; he is free in poverty, and we are free to relate to him in our poverty. Christ-mass is a sign to us of the pilgrim/poverty/suffering axis of the faith we claim is ours.

This is a mystery.

The *future* vision is that this manifestation of God is going to "happen again," not in microcosm (that is, through one isolated child) but through an explosion of consciousness and awareness which encompasses all of the universe and fills it with ultimate meaning. This is the "hope" of Christ-mass, that love—in the radical sense of the ability freely to share life with others without manipulation, exploitation, or bad faith—will pervade and cleanse *all* humanity, the whole creation.

Along with this goes the vision of a radically open social order. Clearly a personal manifesto of love cannot but lead to social consequences, cannot but build its own social consequences. If it doesn't it is being aborted somehow. And it *is* aborted. There are those who construct good family models and then act as if the rest of the world can simply go to hell on a truck, because they no longer care. Only when their children get confronted with the social order, run smack up against the demonic, life-crushing structures in which we live, do they care. Then the cure is adjustment rather than change of the order. You have to "adjust" to the social order; the Christ-mass dynamic of radically open social order, capable of change, is lost. Our consciousness is dimmed. Christ-mass future can help open and raise that consciousness.

This is a mystery.

The community and the individual celebrate the reality of radical love here and now by remembering the past (the birth of Jesus) and by hoping in the future (symbolized in the New Testament and the church's worship as the "Second Coming of Christ" or the "kingdom of God"). They do this in the *present* by celebrating the awareness and love and caring that are already here, in our midst, when we open our eyes.

The failure of the ecclesiastical and secular "Xmas" is that it focuses on the past (relegating Christ-mass to just a historical date, like the Norman Conquest of 1066, which hardly affects us) and thus obscures the present power of Christ-mass. This is the conservative churches' approach to Christian truth: lock it up tight with a small baby in a manger two thousand years away, but give little in the way of handles to get to your own mind or experience. Religion thus becomes an "opiate of the people," rather than a tool by which to raise consciousness and give power for confrontation with the evils of society.

On the other hand, there is that strain in Christianity which focuses its attention almost exclusively on the future of the faith of Christ-mass. This has the practical consequence of denying the reality of our present levels of love, awareness, and confrontation and making a mockery out of our present recognition of God in and through our relationships. For a long time, theological liberalism was tarred with this brush. It is the ecclesiastical equivalent of that old-time Marxism that made the current generation so much fodder for those who would live in the good time coming. Such an approach robs present life of a great deal of meaning and enthusiasm.

Christian celebration of the Christ-mass season must push through the false alternatives and strike a balance. Not only must the past history of the faith be re-created anew, the present experience of love must be undergirded in the hope of expansion into a wider frame of reference, and the future visions must be concretely related to the place where people find themselves here and now. This kind of celebration will take different shapes in different places: of necessity it will look different in a rural parish than in an urban Black church. But the principle of balance needs to remain constant. The radical nature of Christ-mass is regained through emphasizing all three aspects, past, present, and future, at the same time. R. D. Laing has said that there are only two possibilities in response when you confront the reality of experience: horror and hope. Christianity is the record of a confrontation with reality which issues forth in the hope-ful response. We have no option but to build on the response of *hope*, for within our experience, reality is love, and it is not hostile. Concretely within the Christ-mass celebration, hope takes the shape of underwriting present experiences of love and justice; at the same time it opens doors into wider vistas of love and justice for people —in such a way that they can see the progression from where they are to where they can be (because if they cannot, horror is the response and it will lead to despair). Horror should only be the response of those for whom there is no platform of love and justice on which to build forward, of those who have not undergone revolution in their lives. And they deserve to be confronted in the name of the Christ-mass gospel.

It is true that the celebration of Christ-mass in the present is conditioned by "memory" and "hope." These are, however, not restrictive but reflective conditions. If they become restrictive, then radical Christ-mass cannot be unleashed and people will leave the church in droves (which is happening) to seek the experience elsewhere—in drugs, meditation, yoga, you name it. But as *reflective* conditions, "memory" and "hope" lead us to the ultimate questions: What is the meaning of love and caring and awareness—in short, the presence of God—for my life, my relationships, and the world in which I live? Where do they come from? What do I do with them? How do I respond to these gifts?

It is a Christian truth that every man is worthy of dignity and honor, that each individual is sacred and must not be exploited, because he is radically accepted by God. It is the Christian proclamation that now, in this present moment, wherever you are sitting or standing, you can strip to the core of your being and find there not *silence* but a gigantic yes. It is the Christian proclamation that all systems which obscure your love and dampen your awareness are evil because they deny your radical humanity. But so many people get accustomed to and satisfied with being less than human. Like robots in a machine culture, they act *as if* they were human, not because they *are*. Huxley's *Brave New World* provides the scenario for an antiphon to the Christ-mass gospel message. Miller's Willy Loman from *Death of A Salesman* provides the antithetical model to Kazantzakis's deeply visceral Christian *Zorba*. Huxley and the gospel, Willy Loman and Zorba: they all provide models of reality. The question is which one do we operate with? And if we choose to operate with the gospel and Zorba, how do we proclaim/celebrate it now? Christianity has, throughout its history, been an antithetical religion: it has studied the culture and unmasked the demonic in it. Berdyaev spoke of the culture of the world as a kind of "negative revelation" of the truth of Christianity. We need to see this aspect of the culture and use it. Christ-mass reminds us each year to do precisely that . . . in our lives, in our relationships, in our culture.

Radical Christ-mass is the unfolding of a great big yes to man's true experience and yearning and discovery of the divine in himself and in his relationships with others. Radical Christ-mass says no to all systems and institutions and people who want to manipulate and exploit and put others down. Radical Christ-mass says "God is at the center of life, and all of life moves toward the realization of God" when you strip away all the things that numb your ability to receive and give love. Radical Christ-mass says that God is love personified/im-person-ated in this small child of Bethlehem . . . a love which does not jump back into "heaven" but expands throughout all human nature. It is still here, waiting each year, each day, each minute, to be discovered. Christ-mass is the Eternal Now focusing in the temporality of life.

And that, too, is a mystery.

There is no way to a legitimate celebration of Christ-mass without unmasking the demonic structures that veil our eyes from the reality of the human condition. Berne called these structures "games" that we play with one another to keep ourselves from seeing the truth of who we are, confronting it, and altering ourselves in some way to come in closer touch with others in bonds of spontaneity and intimacy. We all play "games." The destructive games have big-sounding names like "international diplomacy," "foreign relations," "civil rights." Radical Christ-mass needs to confront these to open the eyes of people to the fact that sin is the masquerading of reality. Part of the reason Christ-mass falls on its face each year is that we are unable, in our celebration, to cut through the nonsense that masquerades as reality (and which most people accept as reality) to the deeper reality of God. Close attention must be paid to this if the message and experience of Christ-mass are to be proclaimed and celebrated aright in our age.

Some of the existential implications of Christ-mass, then, are:

1. The awareness that reality is incarnational, that grace is possible within the fleshly framework and not apart from it. The awareness that our present experience of love participates in the divine love, which amplifies and fulfills it.

2. The awareness that life is filled with the rhythm of the sacred, that the sacred is not to be found in another "sphere" of life separated from the ordinary. Concomitantly, there is an awareness that the constructs of reality by which we build our models

may, in fact, be masquerades that separate us from reality. Sin is a
mask put upon reality, in this view.

3. The awareness that to seek for God may be never to find him,
because a sought-after God is a God outside the realm of human
experience. The concomitant truth is the ability to wonder and be
surprised by life, which is a prerequisite for the recognition of
God within the main flow of life.

4. The awareness that cosmic hope is at the center of life. To
realize this, one must penetrate or be open to all the possibilities
of existence, and be prepared for the response of horror. When the
Christ-mass meaning is offered, however, we see that hope is the
proper response because the universe is grounded in the reality
of love.

(Note: The Christ-mass celebration that follows has a number
of extra notes in it which will not be reduplicated in the other
liturgical forms. We have made the decision that Advent really
belongs at the end of the revolutionary year, because its proclamation deals primarily with the eschatological inbreaking of
Christ in the "Second Coming" or Parousia. Historically, then,
Christ-mass begins the cycle because it marks the historical root
of the faith. This is debatable, of course, because everyone knows
that Christ-mass is also historically the last festival added to the
church year—with the exception of Trinity Sunday. Easter is the
hinge on which the whole year swings, it is true. But Christ-mass
matches the rhythms of our own lives more with its emphasis on
birth. See almost any book which deals with the technical materials of the seasons [pericopes and propers] and make your own
decision.)

THE MYSTERY MEAL
(Christ-mass to Epiphany)

The mystery of the Christian faith is centered in the Resurrection,
but historically it goes back to the miracle of Christ-mass: God
became man. The amplification of that miracle comes in the

Epiphany season, with its emphasis on the *unveiling* of God in the world of men. This mystery is not something to be intellectually believed only, but to be experienced. Our lives beat to the throb of Christ-mass as we experience love with another person, openness in community, significance in our history-making. Within the community of faith, we celebrate the presence of love in our historical memory of the birth of Jesus and in our present acts of love toward one another. This love is a mystery which the world, blinded as it is by pride and intellectual machinations, cannot perceive. Yet we celebrate this mystery as the power that will overcome the world.

OPENING SONGS
The songs are chosen on the spot by individual members of the community. (At the Community of the Spirit the selection is usually made from the "Getting Started" section of our Celebration Book.) It is up to the liturgical president to gauge the time involved, to sense whether the community wants to keep singing or move into the liturgy proper.

OPENING VERSICLES
    V. Glory to God in the highest!
    R. And on earth peace to men of good will.
    V. Unto us a Child is born, unto us a son is given:
    R. And the government shall be upon his shoulder.
    V. The Lord reigns, he is clothed with majesty:
    R. The Lord is clothed with strength which he has put on.
    V. Behold the Lord, the Ruler, has come:
    R. The Kingdom, the Power, and the Glory are in his hand.
    V. The Lord has revealed his presence to his people:
    R. The Lord will bless his people with peace!
The opening versicles are led by someone from the community.

THE STATEMENT OF PURPOSE *(A short explanation of the theme for the celebration.)*
The statement of purpose replaces the Introit, and serves in its capacity in these services. The statement of purpose can be read by anyone as long as it is written out in advance. The Community of the Spirit, from which these liturgies come, gathers purposes

*about every three months. These purposes come from individuals
in the community and they form the core of the worship celebration for an evening. The pastor of the community coordinates
Psalms and biblical readings with the purpose for the night, and
of course the contemporary word centers in a consideration of
the purpose, too. These purposes are also coordinated with the
historic purposes of the church, especially the saints' days which,
in our liturgical reckoning, take precedence over the purposes
gathered for celebrations from the community. The purposes
gathered from within the community can be looked at in the contemporary word from the thrust of the given season in which they
are used. So, for example, a purpose such as "Is violence justifiable
in a Christian ethic?" celebrated during the Easter cycle would
demand a consideration from the base of the meaning of Resurrection. The purpose is kept very short and is, contrary to the historic Introits, not cast in biblical verses but in contemporary
speech.*

THE PSALM *(Read responsively, verse by verse.)*
*As we mentioned above, it is up to the liturgical president to pro-
vide Psalms which correlate with the purpose for the night, but
the leading of the Psalm is by another member of the community.*

THE FREE PRAYER *(Community response:* "For Christ was born to
bring us peace and love.")
*The free prayer is exactly what its name suggests. Whoever leads
the free prayer should have one or two petitions that he/she can
open with. It is up to the rest of the community to bring their
petitions here. The petitions should be short and specific. At the
conclusion of the free prayer the leader may end with the following
two petitions:* "May all our words be turned into actions in daily
life" *and* "May the prayers which remain unspoken in our hearts
find an answer." *After this he/she should say* "Amen" *to signal
the close.*

READINGS *(Other readings first; biblical readings last.)*
*The readings come from the community, and really the term
"reading" can be misleading, since we encourage people to bring*

posters to show, songs to sing, etc. The criterion on which readings are brought by individuals is clear: whatever you find to relate to what is sacred in your life is fair game to bring as a "reading." Following all other readings, the biblical readings are read by an individual from the community.

THE CONTEMPORARY WORD

The word is normally the domain of the liturgical president. If a "sermon" is offered within the celebration, it is very short—usually no more than five minutes. Time is given to contemplate its meaning. We try to prepare "sermons" for which the primary response will be only deep contemplation and thought. Sermons are usually given in conjunction with purposes related to the revolutionary year seasons or the saints' days, for fairly obvious reasons. The function of the sermon in this kind of celebration is clearly only to proclaim the mystery which is the purpose for the celebration, not to encounter intellectual arguments or serve as a didactic sounding board. Usually, however, sermons are not given; the format is an open dialog, with the liturgical president—or someone else who wants to prepare for it—giving maybe a two or three minute introduction of the topic under discussion. These discussions frequently enter tangential areas and when they do we close them off because their power is dissipating. On occasion we have used films as the basis for discussion, too. Here it is up to the discretion of the community and its liturgical president.

THE AFFIRMATION

When the time was ripe,
God appeared in the mainstream of man.
He came, not with the lightning bolt
nor with the clamor of kingship
nor midst the applause of all mankind.
He came, still and small,
into the poverty of the world,
perceived only by the heart of man.
We are those who celebrate his coming
in time at the manger of Bethlehem.
We are the shepherds who kneel before Him.

We are the wise men who bear gifts to Him.
In the Christ child we see the mystery
of God made plain in the world of men,
A mystery which we know in our hearts
and which we celebrate in our meal.
Gather us together again, O Christ,
through your meal and your word and
through the love we bear each other.
Gather us as the community of peace,
as we celebrate your coming in time.

The affirmation is led by an individual member of the community.

MORE SONGS

THE OFFERING PERIOD *(Pick out your self-offering for the coming week: something you will do or not do—and reflect on it. Ask yourself how you can give of yourself to celebrate the truth of Christmass with others.)*

The offering period is a period of silence, of course. If desired, a plate may be passed around symbolically to signify that each person offers something of himself in the spreading of the gospel. The period of silence need not be long.

THE EXTENSION OF THE COMMUNITY
   1. *announcement of any coming events*
   2. *statement of purpose for the next celebration*
   3. *introduction of newcomers to the community*

Individuals may bring announcements of projects of social outreach, etc., for this part of the service. It is a time of recognition of those who are new. And the giving of the purpose for the coming celebration assists people in looking for the materials they want to bring which are somewhat coordinated with it.

SONG BEFORE THE COMMUNION LITURGY *(optional)*

THE MYSTERY MEAL

   THE RECONCILIATION PERIOD *(Face-to-face discussion to begin, renew, or work on relationships with others. Share hang-ups where possible; speak to the heart of the person you are with; open yourself up and know that Christ is present in your communication with one another.)*

The reconciliation period is one of the most dramatic parts of the small-group liturgy. The liturgical president must sense when the conversations of people are breaking down, when they are drifting into extraneous matters. This is meant as a beginning for people who are having trouble relating to one another. It not infrequently happens that people must be given time to go off and work on the problems in another part of the house before they return to the service. The liturgical president can offer a concluding general Absolution if he so desires.

THE KISS OF PEACE *(sharing on an affectional level)*
    V. Christ is born!
    R. God is present in our community and its love.

The kiss of peace is shared among all present. This can be a lengthy part of the service, because people will want to share the peace with everyone present instead of perfunctorily passing it from one person to the next.

THE SONG BEFORE THE MEAL *(optional)*
This is helpful to bring everyone back together before the meal itself. Since there is a disparity of time in people finishing the Kiss of Peace, those who sit down first can begin a song and others will join in before the eucharistic prayer.

The eucharistic action consists of four movements: taking, blessing, breaking, and giving. Taking refers to the presentation of bread and wine as signs of our work. Blessing is the Thanksgiving Prayer which is written out below. Breaking: the loaf is broken, the wine is poured out, to show the sacrificial nature of love. Giving refers to sharing the meal.

THE THANKSGIVING PRAYER
We give thanks to you O God our Father, whom we know as our Father through Jesus Christ your Son. In and through Him we receive adoption as sons of God who hear and keep the Word. We give you thanks for your loving-kindness toward us and your preservation of all creation.

Chiefly, however, we give thanks for the gift of your Son, Jesus of Nazareth whom we call Christ and Lord. In Him we see the mystery of Divinity in the form of man; through Him mankind is raised to receive God. He is the channel through whom the mystery of God in the world is revealed. We see in Him the manifestation of all that man may become, all that God may be; we live toward that reality as we join in the meal which he celebrated to create the new human community. On the night of his betrayal, he took bread, gave thanks, and broke it and gave it to his disciples saying, "Take and eat: this is my body which is given for you. In like fashion he took the cup when he had drunk from it, gave thanks and offered it to them saying, Drink of this, all of you: this cup is the new covenant in my blood, poured out for you and for many for the remission of sins. Do this often, as you think of me."

It is through the Spirit that we are called and gathered into the new human community begun with the birth of Christ. Spirit of the Living God, be present with us now; accept our gifts of bread and wine, accept us as we come together here and now; bless these gifts and bless our lives for service in peace and love. To God alone be glory and honor forever and ever! Amen.

THE OUR FATHER

V. As often as we eat this bread and drink this wine:
R. We show forth the Lord's death until he comes.
V. Celebrate the mystery of our Lord's coming in time.
R. Let the community demonstrate the mystery of his coming!

THE MYSTERY MEAL

In the sharing of the meal, the president passes first the bread with the words, "N_____, the bread of love, the Body of Christ," which the person then repeats to the one next to him and so on; then the wine is passed with the words, "The cup of blessing, the Blood of Christ," and so on. Needless to say, this formula is only a suggestion.

TIME FOR SILENT REFLECTION *(How can the meaning of Christ's birth for us be more clearly demonstrated in the world, beginning with me?)*

THE CLOSING THANKSGIVING PRAYER *(By a member of the community.)*

CLOSING SONGS
THE BLESSINGS

> V. Shall we thank the Lord once more?
> R. Yes, we'll thank him once again.
> V. Thanks be to God.
> R. Thanks be to God, who came to men in Christ.
> V. Go forth with joy and peace.
> Live as men of good will and of peace.
> You have seen the coming of the Lord.
> Create the community of the Lord where you can.
> Deepen your relationships with all men.
> In the name and for the sake of Christ.
> R. So be it. So shall we live!

The formal verbal input in these liturgies is very minimal, as is obvious. It could, of course, be cut down even less, but we have found that the few added versicles and responses during the service help to demonstrate more clearly the nature of the liturgy. They also help to keep us plugged in to the seasonal thrust during the year. The variety in these liturgies is provided by the individual input, so that despite their patterned similarity and retention of the liturgical format, they are a unique and different experience each time they are celebrated.

WE HAVE ALWAYS LIVED ON THIS MOUNTAIN
or, what would have happened had Peter had his way

In these parts it is simply taken for granted:
We have always lived on this mountain.
Oh, of course, we sometimes go down—
down into the midst of the crowd;
but the people make us feel so confined.
They watch us with hawk eyes
waiting for the little slip of the tongue
at which they can wag their heads
and cluck their tongues and say "unh hunh!"
Or else they simply ignore us altogether
choosing to act as if we didn't exist
Acting to choose that we didn't exist
And so we go back up the mountain.

It is our mountain, all right.
On it we never get hurt.
We never even *feel* bad.
We live such a good life on our mountain
Never having to argue or fuss
Never becoming involved with "them"
Taking life oh so seriously
And passing down many judgments
for which our position of superiority
has so nobly and aptly fitted us.
Yes indeed we love our mountain.

We have a great deal of trouble with people . . . but then
In these parts it is simply taken for granted
that we shall always live on this mountain.

3

EPIPHANY AND
SUBJECTIVITY

Christ-mass is an occasion for three celebrations. The first is the birth of Jesus, the carpenter of Nazareth; this was a rather obscure historical occurrence, little noticed by the people among whom Jesus was born, little noticed by the forces, the systems, the ideologies of his time, little noticed by the religious or secular men among whom he came. He grew, a man among men, in order that he might exhibit something deep within the world of men; in order that he might exhibit a sensitive love toward humanity, toward the creation, and toward God.

The second celebration is the humanity of God; the im-personation of God in a man, a man precisely like you and me, a man who had joys and cares and sorrows; a baby who squalled and screamed in his crib. The humanity of God: God, not off in an obscure heaven somewhere, but *within* the world and life of men.

The third celebration comes because Christ-mass is an occasion for thanksgiving. All of the intimations of men about love and peace before the time of Christ are realized in the person of Jesus. The concept of love has really been born; and that is the meaning of Christ-mass. Love, real love, is to be found beginning from the manger at Bethlehem. It is to multiply thousandfold among men.

Following this threefold celebration comes the next season for celebration in the revolutionary year: Epiphany.

Epiphany has, for centuries, been denied a real place in the revolutionary year. Perhaps we are embarrassed over the festival and its season, embarrassed because of its mystery and mysticism. Embarrassed because it seemingly has little to do with man and a great deal to do with "God," the divine in the midst of the world. We of the West have a great difficulty coping with the divine. Our rational nature focuses on the minutiae of doctrine but fails in the contemplation of divinity. We have rejected the mystical tradition in most Western Christianity, particularly in Protestantism, and this has colored our whole approach to religious experience. It is not without significance that Epiphany has always held a place of honor within Eastern Christianity. We need to learn from the East to shut our mouths before the mysterious presence of divinity, which is what Epiphany is all about. In some ways, it may deserve the title, because of the lessons for the season, of "the season of silent mystic contemplation."

We spoke of Christ-mass as the time for celebrating the birth of Jesus, the humanity of God, the occasion for thanksgiving. To contrast this with Epiphany, we need to note that Epiphany turns all these celebrations round and views them from the other side. The celebrations of Epiphanytide indicate more about God than about man. If Christ-mass is the celebration of the humanity of God, then Epiphany is the celebration of the divinity in man, focused in the paradigm-man, Jesus.

Men of all ages have said, "I can see Jesus as the good teacher; I can understand him as a good man, a real man among men; I can see that many of the things he said would make for a good moral code. Jesus is basically the good teacher, the rabbi; the one who comes to us and indicates a way of life which will reveal to us what God is all about." While this may contain a great deal of truth, it is not the whole truth of the gospel, and the Epiphany season is the safeguard within the revolutionary year that plainly states it is not the whole truth.

People have often found it hard to accept Jesus' divinity. Paul was aware of this problem when he spoke of the "scandal of the cross"; some theologians have called it the "scandal of particularity." How can divinity be in this man Jesus? Yet people are searching for the mystery and awe and sense of wonder that make up an experience of the holy; they deny divinity to Jesus but seek it in many other places—in astrology, the occult, or within the framework of Eastern religions.

Epiphany is meant to focus our minds and hearts on the divinity in Jesus. Even if we cannot yet accept it (what is the meaning of "acceptance" here? It really means to be overwhelmed by the truth of the Incarnation), Epiphany means to tell us that in this man Jesus of Nazareth God was very definitely to be found.

The problem of Western Christianity, which clouds our celebration and witness, is that we are unwilling to see Jesus as a *model*; we are unwilling to accept our own religious experience as being related to his. We have excluded the incarnational principle from all mankind and given it only to Jesus. Hence, Epiphany in the West, rather than offering strength and fire to the individual Christian, makes God terribly remote and Jesus remarkably unreal.

The opening chapter of John speaks of the coming of the Word. There is a word of peace, a word of liberation, a word of love, a word of justice and reconciliation among men. This Word is divine; and this Word is in the world, but the world does not completely perceive it. The world is blinded to its meaning. Jesus' place was to *be* this Word of God to man, and only secondarily the teacher of insights about God. The Word of God to man, within mankind. This is what Epiphany celebrates among us, even when individually we cannot yet celebrate it. This is what we celebrate who can celebrate it: the coming of the Word. God in human form. Divine nature in human nature, beginning with the model, Jesus, whom we (for this reason) call the Christ. An occasion for celebration. An occasion for wonder.

The Epiphany season has the overall purpose of raising our consciousness to perceive the presence of God in the world of man. Historically, the church has used three texts to proclaim this: the visit of the wise men, the miracle at Cana, and the baptism of Jesus. Epiphany says to us that God is openly present within humanity; that God is to be found in the material things of life, that God is found in the "space" between you and me when we deeply share and care for one another; Epiphany points to Jesus as the bearer of this divinity, and proclaims that all manifestations of love beyond him relate back to him as the model (1 John 4:19). This is an open mystery; it is proclaimed, it is spoken and acted through the ages in the liturgy of the church. It is in the open for anyone to perceive who has the eyes to see and for anyone to understand who has the ears to hear.

But Epiphany, at the same time, does remain mystery. Despite the fact that it is open for investigation in the realm of experience within your life (so-called soft data), Epiphany remains a mystery. You can intellectually comprehend the truth: "God is love. Love has come into humanity." But until you perceive it on the level of cosmic wisdom, on the level of mystic insight, it remains unreal; it remains a mental construct, not an organizing principle for the whole of life.

So the wise men are signs to us: signs that the place to which we may continually turn, if we are to understand the centrality of love, is the model of Jesus. In his life we find the meaning of "God is love"; in his life we find the traces which correlate to our own experience of love as the organizing reality of life.

Within our celebration, we need to recapture the sense of mystery, especially during the Epiphany season. There is no clear way to do this; each community of Christ must find its own way to deal with the mystery without losing it in rationalism. At the Community of the Spirit we celebrate the Mystery Meal, a meal designed for use in both the Christ-mass and Epiphany seasons; it has both sides of the coin, as it were, of Christ-mass and Epiphany. We use much more silence; we contemplate the texts rather than rattling on verbally about them (so much chatter in the skull separates us from God anyway); we consciously seek out the signs of love between us as the presence. To the observer's eye, it would appear that the liturgical life is about the same as at other periods. But the internal attitude of the celebrants is different; it is keener; there is more sensitivity to the divinity of the world and of individual men whom God has given us in this community. We burn more incense, light more candles, sing a few more songs. All of these things are external signs of the inner search to appreciate the mystery of the divine-human character of the world.

Classical Christian catechisms speak of the threefold office of Christ as that of prophet, priest, and king. Epiphany is the season of the revolutionary year that celebrates Christ *officially* as prophet, priest, and king. The visit of the wise men is an indication of his kingship, and their homage to him shows that allegiance to Christ surpasses allegiance to the emperor and everything else because it points us beyond the temporality and death of the systems and institutions around us to the infinity and ultimacy of God.

The baptism of Christ speaks of his office as prophet. His baptism shows that he is identified with the people among whom he works and lives. He identifies himself with their joys and sorrows; he identifies himself with the religious tradition. He relates himself to the concerns that plague man while pointing to the centrality of God in life.

The second identification of Jesus in the baptism is with the entire historical process of God. By this we mean that Jesus of Nazareth reaffirms the ways in which God has previously demonstrated his presence. His model is not an anarchistic break with the past; nor is it simply an evolutionary development from the past. His emphasis is on an appropriation of the past, a correction of its abuses in his own person, and a revolutionary penetration to the depth of its meaning. He identifies with the historical process of God.

The key words in the baptismal texts are those that indicate the pleasure of God with this special son. So it is a declaration of Jesus as the prophet, the one who is the mouthpiece of God, the one who proclaims the word of God, the one who bears the word of God to man. The text says to us that Jesus does this in a very special way, that there is something new here which goes beyond the prophets of the Old Testament. He not only bears the word of God to men as prophet, but he is *the* prophet who is the Word of God to men. His baptism says to us that, beginning with this man, God's Word is to be found in the crucible of human action. He is ordained for service; he is set apart to *be* for us the prophetic Word of God.

The perception of God within the mean and the ordinary events of the creation, within the flow of human life, may seem like the most difficult thing in the world. It seems as if we are faced with a barrier all the time. If we define God as love, understand his nature this way, and then try to develop loving relationships, surely we ought to find God in the midst of these relationships. But that is not always true; our love falls short, our relationships wither, intimacy fails us in our contracts and commitments as they grow old and unfortunately stale. We conclude: "God is apparently not present here. Therefore, God can't be present here. Therefore, there is no God."

This is a perplexing situation; it is a situation around us everywhere. Those who are not sure of God try to break through to a god through drugs, through meditation, through "success" in their own existence (whatever that means), through justifying their own existence by the things they do, rather than finding themselves in who they *are*.

The text for the miracle at Cana (John 2) is a parable for this situation. It is a parable in the form of a miracle in which Jesus transforms water into wine. But the real transformation that is taking place is that of the world. The world is being transformed into a richer, fuller place to live. And Jesus is the priest of this transformation.

The function of the priest is to be the one who stands between God and man, the one by whose sacrifice a fellowship is demonstrated between God and man—in which man begins to receive the gifts of divinity in terms of personal freedom and dignity, in terms of responsibility and identity, in terms of sensitivity and awareness of the meaning within the world, and God in turn is viewed no longer as judge, but as the Father of mankind who lives in a relationship of love to his children.

The New Testament associates the fullness of this priesthood with Jesus of Nazareth (see especially the Epistle to the Hebrews). The New Testament confirms what we already know inside ourselves: we cannot break through to God—to peace and wholeness, to reality—unless God breaks through to us. Jesus is the "man in the middle," the priest in this process, who continually offers man up to God and offers God up to man, that they might meet each other. The doctrine of the divine-human natures in Christ is the intellectual model the church has coined for this process. But the experience rests "below the mind." Epiphany is the season that tells us of the beginning of the interflow of divinity and humanity in our high priest, Jesus.

The Epiphany season closes in our tradition with the Transfiguration. No more mysterious festival is found within the church's revolutionary year. Here we see Jesus unmasked; he is "superior" to the tradition of the legal approach to God (represented by Moses) and "superior" to the tradition of the prophetic approach to God (represented by Elijah.) The Transfiguration is a mystery for our contemplation, not a logical compilation of data for our intellect to reason through. Just as it was a mystery for the contemplation of Peter, James, and John, the so-called inner circle of disciples who were present at this event. This is an event which takes place on the interior of man, when we realize the significance and the power of the person of Christ. The Epiphany season needs to be shaped so that this significance, this power, can be apprehended by those who celebrate with us.

If Christ-mass is the time for celebrating objective reality, Epiphany matches it (and by so doing, matches the human need to internalize objective data and give it existential meaning) by forcing us to contemplate and think about our *own* experience, in order that we can subjectivize the truth within us and find the presence of God in all the contemporary moments of the world.

We thus see three existential themes for this season:

1. The awareness of the cosmic nature of love. Love is the central force in the universe; this love is coming into the world, mediated by the priesthood of the paradigm, Jesus the Christ.

2. The awareness of the transcendent potential wtihin everyday events, shown by the miracle at Cana. The sanctification of the commonplace is a key theme during Epiphany. This awareness matches the experience of man that certain aspects of his

life are elevated above the level of the commonplace: the perception of beauty in the world, the touch of love, and so on.

3. The awareness of the process by which divinity enters humanity. Divinity does not enter the mainstream of human experience from the outside, but is the depth within it.

ON BEGINNING LENT AGAIN

Part of the pain of my life
Is to be found in the fact
That I recognize Lent's meaning.
I recognize within all of life
A deeper meaning which is Christ
In an age which doesn't give
A tinker's damn for Christ.
I want to be the church where I am,
reshape and remold it anew
For an age which thinks it passé.
Herein lies the pain of my life,
That—knowing Christ's reality—
I cannot communicate it in ways
which make a big difference
For a large number of people.
I don't want to be big, really,
But I want Christ and his Church
To be recognized as power and life.
In the midst of Lent stands a cross
reminding us of the success of failure
Showing us power in powerlessness.
Part of the pain of my life
Is to be found in all of this,
For I fail by my powerlessness.
The suffering must be worth it.

4

LENT:

LOOK INSIDE YOURSELF

The next season of the revolutionary year is called Lent. It is a time of reflection. It is a time to recapture some of the ground you think you have lost in the rush of life. Lent is the church year season which appears, on the surface, to have least to do with daily life. But this is not a true judgment; Lent belongs not as an addition to the meaning of life but as a part of the search for depth and meaning within life. It is a time of testing, a time for reflection upon the direction of your life.

The prophet Amos spoke of a time when life would be barren and void because the word of God would be absent from it (Amos 8:11–12). He understood the word to be the creative power of God, the power that holds the universe together and carries it through history. On a more personal level the word may be seen as the power which drives men forward in their lives to find joy, to overcome hardship, to bend and change their world, to actualize themselves. When that word is lost, everything is lost. Life's meaning is gone. To a degree, the world is always caught in a time of no-word. It is not that the word is really gone, but the ability to comprehend it seems to be missing. Men search for new ways of life, when in fact the radical message of the gospel—the liberating, freeing word of God that both creates and sustains life—still beats beneath all the nonsensical ways we try to comfort ourselves or dull ourselves to problems, or simply escape from the exigencies of life altogether.

The Christian is a person who sees in Jesus of Nazareth a turning point in history, when the Word of God comes into the world in human nature—never to leave it again, never to be gone from the world. The meaning of Christ opens up in our lives as we unmask the evils of the world, confront them, see them as they really are. It opens up when we see another person in the unitive light of love, perhaps for the very first time. It opens up when we achieve real communication, for that is surely part of the Word of God.

It is this mystery that we are called to reflect, not as an addition to our lives, but where and when we find it in our lives. Lent is the season which offers the renewal of our religious experience of love and truth and unity, which calls us to gather together the bits and pieces of our experience and see it as a whole, in the light of the passion of Jesus the Christ.

Lent is for Christians. Like the Sermon on the Mount, it is not intended for open practice. It is specifically for those who find themselves in a relationship to Jesus whereby they see him as the Lord of their lives. It is for those who have committed themselves to continuously opening up the meaning of the Christ-event for their lives. It has the character of an underground teaching, not to be practiced publicly for show. Even the Lord's Prayer, that most vocal of prayers in Christianity, occurs within a context which suggests it as an underground practice of the Christian, not as a display of religiosity.

The three traditional practices of Lent are: almsgiving, prayer, and fasting. Let us consider the rationale for these in our day. *Almsgiving:* The concern of the church with the poor, the oppressed, the downtrodden, the sick, is not an option but an imperative—an imperative to get on with the task of humanizing the world in the name of God. The poor are not assisted only by words about Jesus; they are assisted by reorganizing the world to give them what they, as human beings, deserve: room to grow and move.

We give not to show we are better than others; we give to assist others to reach a new standard of humanity, a new growth in their lives. We give, not in a patronizing way, as did the hypocrites of Jesus' day who made a big deal of it. The Christian doesn't expect honors and rewards for his almsgiving. When we do give out of a feeling of superiority, it would be better for us and the people we are trying to "help" if we kept our money and our mouths and our minds to ourselves. The poor and the oppressed probably can teach us more than we can teach them, because they know out of their life-condition who they are. Those of us with money and power in the eyes of the world lose sight of who we really are. For these reasons, the church reminds us during Lent of almsgiving in the spirit of the Sermon on the Mount.

Prayer: Noise is one of those things by which we deliberately pollute our minds to keep from coming to grips with questions like, "Who am I? Where am I going? What is the shape of my life?" Even our words can get in the way of looking inside ourselves. This is why Jesus suggests that we shut ourselves off from noise and nonsense and get down to prayer in quiet.

Much of our prayer life, if we have any left, gets off to a false start; it rests on false presuppositions. Any God whom we can manipulate by our words doesn't really have much power or purpose. Similarly, any God whom I call on only in time of need must be a rather depressed God. Prayer as conversation with the divine at the center of your life has a good deal of meaning, but some of our infantile notions about prayer have simply got to go, or else we won't be able to pray at all.

Prayer is not only a conversation with God, but a means whereby we catch our breath in life, look into the future, and seek new vistas for our experience, our growth, and our service. Prayer is, for the new Christian, a means whereby he can stop dying a little through neglecting his own growth or service to his fellowman. It is a time to sensitize oneself to the needs of the world and our selves. The Lenten prayer discipline is a wise commendation; it helps us search ourselves in order that we might stretch ourselves.

Fasting: I remember in 1966 when I helped organize the Holy

Week Fast in Pittsburgh to show concern about the War in Vietnam, I was just beginning to see the rationale behind the Lenten fast. At that time I realized that fasting within the Christian tradition is a means of reminding ourselves of the imbalance in the world's food supply, which is one of the key causes of war. We have, they do not; they want and go to war, and suddenly because they would prefer to have their children live rather than die, they become the enemy, the aggressor. We, with our rounded stomachs, oppose the thin men of the world, frequently citing the name of God as justification for our holy struggle. The Lenten fast reminds us that food is taken for granted among us, while for four-fifths of the world it is a luxury. At the same time, the fact that we can fast as a luxury, as a means of religious commitment, ought be a reminder to us of how well off we are. Others fast of necessity; to us is given the privilege of fasting to show concern.

Fasting is a means of identification with the poor of the world in the name of God; but it also has another character. The body has a need to purify itself, to cleanse itself, in order that the mind can continue to function and not get bogged down by too many riches and too much excess. Fasting offers us the opportunity to hone our minds as well as our bodies.

Yet none of our fasting is worth much if it is done as a show, as Jesus said (Matthew 6). If you are going to fast, don't do it because your church says you must and don't do it to show how "Christian" you are; do it because you need to sharpen your consciousness to see the real condition of the world and the imbalance that exists among the nations.

These are the "externals" of Lent, the disciplines that are offered us by the liturgical round of the year. They have an internal meaning related to the flavor of the whole season. The central theme in Lent is *passion*.

Christianity is a curious religion; not only is it the most materialistic of the religions of the world, it is also the one most clearly concerned with the suffering that the world brings. This is because we have a model for suffering in the Christ of Lent, the passionate, suffering, sympathetic Christ of the road from

Jericho to Jerusalem to Golgotha. He has given us a sign for life, that all growth takes place through pain, that all healing requires suffering, that all life emerges from death. The Christ of Lent illustrates the passion of God. Lent is the time for reflection on that fact. Lent is a time for restructuring our own lives so that they conform to the "mind of Christ," as Paul called that total way of life which is Christianity.

There have been those who again this century have taught us the redemptive shape of suffering: Mahatma Gandhi, A. J. Muste, Martin Luther King, Jr., Dietrich Bonhoeffer, the Berrigans, and others. They have taught us that in suffering for the ills of the world, or for your part in those ills, there comes a form of joy which cannot come in any other way. They have shown us that it is better to die for truth than to live for falsehood, threat, and insecurity. There is something in suffering that straitens us, that puts our minds and hearts into a spirit of receptivity that we cannot get any other way, that puts us into a frame of living which turns us away from selfishness to the concerns and needs of others. This is *right* suffering.

Passion is the original word, from which we get other words such as sym-pathy, em-pathy, and com-passion. Passion is a driving force within you to share life with others and to share in the lives of others, so that together you might realize a more complete world. Jesus of Nazareth was a passionate man; his words and deeds reflect his passionate character. He suffered with the downtrodden; he was joyful with the joyous. By his life he changed lives. In this season of Lent, we are called—through reflection, through the disciplines—to reconsider the direction of our own lives.

The cross is the fulfillment of Lent. It shows the character of God, the passionate character of the God within life, who suffers out of love. All passion is hallowed through this cross; all compassion is raised a notch above the commonplace. The cross is a mystery of the highest rank; it is not possible to explain it. But the shape of love is cruciform; all love is judged by its ability to be compassionate. In the cross, the union between man and God is seen to be the interchange of suffering love. The extension of the cross into all of life is made possible by the passionate love we bear for others; "completing in our own lives the sufferings of Christ." The cross is not the end; it is the consummation of love, the fulfillment of real love.

Lent is a special time for Christian communities. It involves a multiplicity of services, some of which are added to emphasize the character of reflection in the season. At the Community of the Spirit we celebrate the Suffering Meal during this period, a meal calculated to sensitize us to the needs of the community and to cause us to reflect at the same time.

We begin the period by celebrating Shrove Tuesday and Ash Wednesday together. We have an Agape Feast, built around the Eucharist, to which community members bring food, bread, wine. It is a joyous time; there is a lot of laughter. As the clock passes midnight, we shift the mood. The Ash Wednesday pericopes are read, time is given for reflection on their meaning, then the ancient practice of marking the forehead with ashes is explained. As we sing a song of dedication, all those who wish to be marked with ashes file past and are greeted with, "Receive this cross of ashes as a sign that you voluntarily take upon yourself the Lenten period of reflection on suffering, your own and that of Jesus the Christ. Dust you are, and dust shall you return." We have found this a meaningful way to enter the season. This is also the only season during which a cash offering is received. Its use is determined by the community for a special project having to do with the alleviation of human suffering. Information is given about the project, which is determined by the community as a whole, and people are asked to acquaint themselves with its work and help as they can.

The inner attitude sought during the Lenten period is one of reflection on where you are going in life, what the character of your life is, what the place of passion is in your life, how passion is a mark of the presence of God, how you can use your life as a tool to build the new human community. There is a hushed atmosphere in our celebrations during the Lenten period which is natural; it is not impressed from the outside.

Lent matches the need people have periodically to objectify

their lives and their experience to see where they are going. Lent
is the revolutionary year's period for life-planning, for looking at
the *Gestalt* of one's life to try to get some handles on the direction
it is taking.

Lent is traditionally the period of "repentance." Repentance
is, however, only a possibility if we can objectify our existence to
see where it needs revision, change, alteration. For repentance is
change, radical change of mind, of attitude. The process of Lent
should assist people in looking at their experience, reevaluating
it, and in trying to enter the depth of passion for the world, the
passion which is a sign of the presence of love.

Among other things, then, the existential framework of Lent
includes:

1. The awareness that there are forces in the world which
deny personhood, and that each man must enter into the world
with passion to overcome those forces in his own relationships.

2. The awareness that one's own life may not be open to the
divine, because the risk of loving is not carried through to the
end of passionate self-giving.

3. The awareness that sensitivity is needed to confront the
structures that deny humanity.

4. The awareness that suffering *with* someone is frequently the
risk of love, but that we have a model for this suffering which is
not a loss of life, but a triumphant overcoming of evil within life.

THE SUFFERING MEAL
(The Lenten Season)

Lent is an ancient part of the rhythm of the church year. It is a
time of reflection on our lives—on the negative side of our lives,
the side which puts Christ (and many others like him) on the
cross anew each year. But Lent goes beyond reflection; it is a
time for reflection-leading-to-action in the name of Christ. We
identify with a long history of priests and panhandlers, bishops
and bunglers, who refreshed themselves in the Spirit by reflecting on the meaning of Christ's suffering. Whatever our status in

the community—as a hearer or as one of the committed—we must remember that the main function of celebration is not to instruct us but to tune us in to the divine life. Part of the divine life is suffering—passion for and with others; passion within oneself.

OPENING SONGS

OPENING VERSICLES
V. Blow a trumpet in Zion: sanctify a fast.
R. Call a solemn assembly; gather the people.
V. That I may know Christ and the power of his resurrection:
R. That I may share in his sufferings, becoming like him in his death:
V. I count all things—all institutions, all allegiances, all lesser forms of security—as so much garbage.
R. We will not lay up for ourselves treasures on earth.
V. For the sake of Christ's Body, let us rejoice in suffering:
R. By it we complete what still remains to be done to create the new human society.

THE STATEMENT OF PURPOSE

THE PSALM

THE FREE PRAYER (Community response: "Come, Christ, with the burning passion that brings new life to man.")

READINGS (Other readings first; biblical readings last.)

THE CONTEMPORARY WORD

THE AFFIRMATION
Suffering is a trust.
To suffer with another in pain
Is to enter a new relationship.
Suffering is a gift.
To be sensitive to the world's pain
Is the first step toward action.
Suffering is redemptive.
To live through a time of trial
Without losing hope gives new depth to life.
Suffering is with and from God.

To see through a troubled condition
Is to see through to the face of God.
All suffering is a testimony
To the healing power of Christ.
We joyfully accept, within our lives,
That suffering which brings about
The creation of the new community:
The community of the Spirit—
Who leads us into all the truth;
The community of the Christ—
Who leads us all into new life;
The community of the Father—
Whose love is echoed in our lives.

MORE SONGS

THE OFFERING PERIOD *(In this liturgy, there will be a money offering, which will be used for a particularly crucial issue dealing with oppression or poverty. In addition, pick out your self-offering for the coming week—something you will do or not do—and reflect on it.)*

THE EXTENSION OF THE COMMUNITY
  1. *announcement of any coming events*
  2. *statement of purpose for the next celebration*
  3. *introduction of newcomers to the community*

SONG BEFORE THE COMMUNION LITURGY *(optional)*
THE SUFFERING MEAL

THE RECONCILIATION PERIOD *(Face-to-face discussion to begin, renew, or work on relationships with others. Share hang-ups where possible; speak to the heart of the person you are with; know that God is present in your speaking one to another.)*

Conclusion spoken by liturgical president, after which the response:

R. As we open up to the suffering of others, so we feel the presence of Christ, who with his love burns out suffering.

THE KISS OF PEACE *(sharing on an affectional level):*

V. Salute one another with a holy kiss.

R. Christ is in the midst of us!

THE SONG BEFORE THE MEAL *(optional)*

THE THANKSGIVING PRAYER

We give you thanks, Our Father, for the many opportunities you have given us to serve those in need. Forgive any patronizing or paternalism on our part and help those who are in need to see you in the service we render. May we see beneath all suffering to the root of suffering in the systems founded on greed and violence, and let us work to alter such systems. We thank you especially for the gift of Jesus Christ, whose passionate life offers us a model by which to enter into the sufferings of others and become truly compassionate. In his life he exemplified the value of suffering and passion, and by his death that testimony was sealed for all time as the true display of creative love. In order to equip the community of those who co-suffer with the world, in the night of his betrayal, he took bread, and when he had given thanks he broke it and gave it to his community, saying, "Take and eat: this is my body which is broken for you." In similar fashion he took the cup and, after drinking, he blessed it and gave it to them, saying, "Take and drink of this, all of you: this cup is new human society in my blood, which is shed for you and for many for the forgiveness of sins. Do this often, in memory of me."

Send your Spirit upon these humble gifts and into our waiting lives that we might be transformed into vehicles of love for the freeing of the captives and the opening of the prisons of the poor, the lonely, and the alienated. All glory be to you, our Father, and to the Lamb and to the Spirit, forever. Amen.

THE OUR FATHER

 V. As often as we eat this bread and drink this cup:

 R. We show forth the Lord's death until he comes.

 V. Celebrate the mystery of Christ's suffering:

 R. May his passionate love burn out evil through our work!

THE SUFFERING MEAL *(Share with your brother or sister with the words,* "N_____, the bread of suffering, the Body of Christ," *when passing the bread, and* "N_____, the cup of blessing, the Blood of Christ," *when passing the cup.)*

THE CLOSING THANKSGIVING PRAYER *(By a member of the community.)*

CLOSING SONGS

THE BLESSINGS

V. Shall we thank the Lord once more?

R. Yes, we'll bless him once again.

V. Thanks be to God.

R. Thanks be to God, who is with us tonight.

V. Go in peace. Go in love.
Watch and work for the final fulfillment of man.
Until that time, create community through passion.
Deepen your relationships with all men.
In the name and for the sake of Christ.

R. So be it! So shall we live!

To become
what I can;
To be now
what I am;
To be present
where I am;
To be conscious
while I can;
To be aware
of who I am
and who you are;
To reach out
for my potential;
To find fulfillment
in a blade of grass
or a certain smile
or a simple touch;
Because Another
has enabled me
to be, I become
all these things . . .
and even more.

5

EASTER:

THE BURST OF LIFE

"Radical" comes from *radix*, the Latin word for the root, the bottom of the matter, the deepest level you can find. People look for roots. We are, in one sense at least, by nature radical. Wherever we live, we drop roots for a while. We need a history which is my-story. We spin webs of relationships beyond the relationships that originally spun us; we create a history out of the raw materials of people and events, times and places.

Easter (the Festival of the Resurrection) is *the* radical Christian festival. All the rest of the revolutionary year revolves around it, like a wheel radiating out from its hub. Easter is radical; it is the root of the Christian faith-system, the deepest level of truth to which you can penetrate; and it is the beginning of the web out of which all Christian history has been built, and continues to be built. It is the "center" of history, because it is the center of community. The relational web is spun by Easter; and the community is built through baptism, which is related to Easter for its origin and meaning. It is the theological center of the church, too; theology in our century has resembled a pendulum swinging back and forth between the poles of objective validity and subjective (existential) meaning. But these are to be held in a creative tension. Objective validity without subjective meaning becomes faith-less content. Subjective meaning without objective validity becomes content-less faith. The Resurrection is the point of merger between these two poles. It is the deepest experience of reality, and at the same time it is the most profound word about that reality.

For the church, the festival of Resurrection is the radical center of the revolutionary year. The West, however, with its emphasis on logic and rationalism, tended to play down Resurrection and became more concerned with what it saw as history (Christmass), because history is calculable, manageable. The theology of the West has also been cross-centered to the extreme, because the cross is (theoretically) more capable of rational explanation than is the Resurrection. These two positions have colored the whole of Western Christianity, just as the centrality of Easter in the Eastern church has colored it as a church of mystery and drama. Recognizing the mystery-character of Easter, what follows in this chapter is not really logical explanation. It is an attempt to convey the mystery.

People experience life-and-death cycles within their own lives. We have recently been conditioned to speaking of "raising consciousness." When this occurs to someone, his experience is often termed a rebirth. I enter a relationship with a person in which I give myself to him/her and he/she gives "self" back to me, and we have created, or birthed, a new thing. $1+1=3$! I enter a deeper level of relationships with my "self" and I find that my "self" is amplified, stretched, maybe a little bit reborn. I enter a different level of relationships with what I consider to be divine and I find my self reborn. Just as there is no growth without pain, so there is no life without death. The Christian faith in Resurrection relates to this personal experience. It is not guaranteed by the experience, but it is the ground out of which the experience can be interpreted. Easter is the fulfillment of experience. It can be seen as a paradigm for all experience of life-and-death.

The concept of human potential is very much in the air today. It refers to the possibility of the individual becoming more fully what he is. The churches are involved in the human potential movement because they see this movement as another in a series of ways to demonstrate the meaning of Christianity. Each step of the process of becoming, of actualizing your potential, involves a change, a dying of the old self, and a little rebirth, a "little Easter" of the new self. The effect is both qualitative and quantitative. We usually perceive it qualitatively: "I'm a different person today than I was yesterday." But it is also quantitative; you grow from where you are to where you're going to be. An acorn doesn't grow up to be a rose; it grows up to be an oak. Each individual grows to become what he potentially is. Easter is the cosmic yes to this existential growth-process, the model for it, the paradigm that shows it in one life.

The Resurrection of Christ is the model for all these kinds of "transforming" or "actualizing" experiences. All our experiences are interpretable by this one Experience (I use the word "experience" with a capital E to denote an event which has three components: objective validity, subjective significance, and the dramatic quality of a landmark or distinctive event which has continuous meaning in the life of the individual). Easter is *the* paradigm of Christianity, which means it is the central interpretation of reality about which all Christianity centers, from which its life-style radiates. Resurrection means freedom: freedom to grow, freedom to expand, room to move. The model is radical. Jesus of Nazareth dies; Christ is resurrected. Actual, literal death precedes the resurrection. Point? Death is an actual fact of life, an inescapable event; but it can no longer trap you in fear, bind you in conformity, chain you to the humdrum existence so many men call "life." How many man-hours of how many counselors have been spent trying to spring people free from fantasized death-fears? The Resurrection of Christ, if you dance to its music, if you hear its beat, says: there is no absolute finality to death; it is robbed of its "sting" (1 Cor. 15:55). Life is process; death is part of the process, not to be fought or feared but to be accepted. The Resurrection says death can be accepted, trusted as part of the process of life out of which new life will come. Jesus is the model for this transformation. All of our transformations relate to his; his transformation relates to all of ours. It is because of the objective Resurrection of Christ that the subjective experience takes on shape and meaning.

Death occurs on many levels other than the physical. Someone is "dead" who is not "alive," that is, who is not actualizing his/ her potential. The opposite of growth is disintegration (loss of integrity). Muscles atrophy when not used. Nothing stays the same. You either go forward or you go backward. There is no such thing as standing still. The reed that tries to stand up straight in the river is broken. Easter has the potential to free the individual for creative living by eliminating the forms of bondage to which our "selves" are chained. Break through all the systems, says Easter. They are illusory values that entrap the mind and stifle the heart, thereby cutting short the creative process of life. Thereby causing death.

Resurrection is experienced in a community of the Resurrection. In such a community, support and affirmation form the bed of history in which individual styles of life are born. All of us need the kind of feedback which assists us to become more who we are. Such feedback opens the channels of creativity again, cuts short the death-process, renews life. On the sociological level, this is what the church as Community-of-Resurrection ought to be: a supportive community in which the unique individual is "raised up" (resurrected). Where this is not happening, "church" does not exist.

On another level, the Resurrection of Christ is the power which creates this community. It is the same power which the community transfers to its members—unless the community is dead. The power is real. The Resurrection is real. It is alive. It is growth-oriented, life-giving, actualizing. Because of the Resurrection/ presence of Christ, a community is born whose members are not frightened by death and who preserve their fellowship without resorting to fear, coercion, or compulsion.

Easter is the wisdom (*sophia*) which the community offers the world. Wisdom here is understood not as metaphysical speculation, not as rational data-collection, not as the accumulation of a body of knowledge, but rather as *mystical intuition*. To speak of Easter as the central Christian mystery is to involve ourselves in such an understanding of wisdom. This is the wisdom of God which is foolishness to the Greeks and a stumbling block to Jews (1 Cor. 1). This is a wisdom which is not possessed; it is rather participated in. No *one* possesses it. Resurrection is never rationally understood; I cannot pass my conceptual framework for Easter from my head to anyone else's and thereby assume that he "believes in Easter." To attempt proofs for it is at most a diversion, if not an exercise in futility. A rational approach to Easter robs it of its proclamatory force. Resurrection is meant for proclamation-as-mystery, not analysis-as-belief.

The Easter message is proclaimed chiefly through a community of the Resurrection. The original "catholicity" of the church is *directly* related to the existential apprehension of the present Christ in a historic community. We had better be clear at this point that there are differences between a "communion" and a "community." A "communion" is a group experience based on emotional insight in which, frequently, the differences between people are smoothed over in a conciliatory fashion rather than acknowledged and worked through. A "communion" brings together, primarily, people who would naturally affiliate with each other because of mutual expectations of each other's behavior. Communion can often be mistaken for community. Most churches are communions, but they are not communities. In a community, people are united on the basis of deeper principles than mutual attraction or commonality of interest. In a Christian community, the core principle is the action of God in the person of Christ, around which people gather to celebrate and work. In such a community, individuality is not lost. People remain true to themselves, but they are changed through the process of identification with the communal models and symbols (creed and liturgy). In a communion, people can lose their individuality and through group-pressure become lost in group-think. The Christian community of the Resurrection is committed to affirming the sanctity of the individual.

The Christian community is founded on the Resurrection. Among the things that this does *not* mean are that it is founded on a rebaptism of the idea of immortality (which is an extension of the attempt to deny death) or simply the existential feeling of birth and rebirth we have discussed above. This is not to say that these concepts are not taken up and utilized, however transformed, within Christianity. It is only to say that they are not determinative for the foundation of the community. The community is founded on the event of the Resurrection, without which it enters life with no meaning. The Resurrection is understood, from this viewpoint as being concrete, complete, and unique. Although it bears mythological overtones, it is not "myth"; it is only that we must use "mythic" terms (terms within space and time) because there are no other terms by which to communicate the mystery of the Resurrection. The church exists as a community to celebrate the Resurrection, and to proclaim and demonstrate its power to the world. The Resurrection stands as the ground out of which the church grows, and the mark which distinguishes it from any other organization.

There are political implications to the Resurrection. Easter unmasks the "rulers of this world" as being oriented to the death-principle. All institutions, systems, ideologies, stand judged in the light of the Resurrection and its promise of life against death. For the power of institutions is their coercive power, their power toward death. This coercion can be experienced in many ways: imprisonment, mental pressure, the threat of punishment for dissent, and so on; but the Resurrection shows that the shape of the Christian community is the shape of *life*. The periods in which the church has been most secure in terms of its faith have been historically the periods in which it has been most insecure over against the society in which it lives. The Resurrection is the force which conveys the simple, but oft-forgotten truth that the Christian is in, but not of, the world. The world's power is that of the sword; allegiance is bought through the threat of violence to the self. Our Easter celebration must be a consciousness-raising device, a tool which clearly demonstrates and celebrates the creation of a new human society in which coercion and violence are no longer the standards for life, but in which life and love are affirmed. This new human society is grounded in the Resurrection. Where it is not, it eventually loses its roots and dissolves into humanism.

The early church celebrated Easter when is gathered for celebration every Sunday. The fact that it moved its day of celebration to Sunday is related to the belief in Christ's Resurrection "on the third day." We need to recapture the Resurrection character of our celebration, with its concomitant joy and hope, peace and love; but we need most assuredly to do this during the season of Easter.

How can we demonstrate the wisdom of Easter, the mystery of the Resurrection, in our celebrations? The following are cast in the way of suggestions and are not meant as any kind of "program":

Maybe Easter needs to be recaptured as the sign of universal unity that it is. The celebration of the Resurrection of Christ is simultaneously the celebration of the unity of mankind. The church needs a self-identity as the new human society, the outpost of a new humanity from which the rest of the world is approached. Each congregation should be imbued with a consciousness of its unique identity as a community of the Resurrection, a community celebrating the unity of a man in Christ.

Maybe Easter needs to be recaptured at its root: freedom from death. Beginning with the freedom from physical death, we must draw out the ramifications of this freedom. We must see it also as freedom from the emotional death of the individual, the death of interpersonal relationships. Something is functionally dead when it no longer plays an active part in anything; in a relationship, a person is functionally dead who is isolated in loneliness. (For the East, isolation is one of the key concepts in the definition of "sin"; its opposite is *sobornost*, community, within which is "salvation.") So when one enters a system of relationships in which it is possible to admit loneliness and isolation, and in which others will respond in love to overcome that loneliness, there the "grace" of Resurrection is seen; the dead are raised to new life. This is no less miraculous than anything recorded in the Gospels. In such a community, people come alive through their love for one another. Luther recognized this when he stated that one of the clear expressions of the gospel is "the mutual exhortation and consolation of the brethren" (*The Smalcald Articles*).

Maybe Easter needs to be recaptured as the base for forgiveness. "Absolution" is the freeing of the individual from his isolation, his alienation—from self, from others, from the world. Within a relationship of love, that alienation is overcome. Dramatic portrayal of this in the liturgy is urgent, because forgiveness is the base for Christian community on the social level. Forgiveness matches Resurrection, which is the base on a cosmic level. The Resurrection shows that the root of the universe is love, that the reality of life is hopeful because reality is love. From this perspective the ancient theologians saw "sin" as something accidental, i.e., something not natural to man. Sin is opposed to faith, which is a relational term. The "sinner" is the individual, the one who has no compassion for his fellowman, who is "unconnected" to any others, who lives in isolation. Viewed on this level, "absolution" is a demonstration of community, whether by one person as representative of the community or by the whole community. This community of the forgiveness of sins must be part of our Easter celebration.

Maybe Easter needs to be seen as the powerhouse which releases the collective energy of the church. Where there is a collective recognition of the unity of mankind, celebrated in microcosm in the congregation, several things can happen.

For one thing, the walls that divide people (roles, institutional affiliations, ideological persuasion) collapse. The existential meaning of the Lordship of Christ comes home with clarity. He is our Caesar; the one to whom we owe primary allegiance. The secondary nature of all ideologies, systems, institutions by which we identify ourselves, or worse, define ourselves, is demonstrated in the Resurrection of Christ. We are shown to be a human community underneath all the debris by which we hold ourselves apart.

For another thing, rather than the individual *losing* himself in the community, his personhood is even more sharply outlined by the affirmation he receives from others. We are affirmed as unique within the community of the Resurrection. The dignity of the individual is an outgrowth of the emphasis on unity and forgiveness, because to have a unity (an I-Thou relationship) you

must see the other as person, unique and sacred in himself, not as
a thing to be manipulated.

The outcome of such celebration should be the release of collective energy. Affirmation is good for the soul. It assists us in
recognizing the power-center in our own lives and utilizing it. It
also assists us in breaking down the barriers we falsely create
between ourselves and others because of the fear of losing ourselves. The Resurrection is the source of this affirmation, and it
must be celebrated as such.

Of course, to take the Resurrection seriously might involve a
radical redesign of our priorities in the church. It might involve
us in looking seriously at what we are doing, dropping those
things which do not make for the creation of an open community,
enhancing all those things that do. It might involve us in the
utilization of methods developed in other sciences than theology
(such as human relations training) in order to communicate the
mystery of the Resurrection and its power for life. It might involve us in some radical political decisions. But the church is
called to be true to the Resurrection; this is its charter and we
cannot abandon it.

A NOTE ON THE ASCENSION. Although the Ascension is theo-
logically one with the Resurrection, it does mark a special celebration within the revolutionary year. There are four notes which
can be made in reference to the Ascension and its little cycle in
the year, which deepen the understanding of Easter.

The first note is the universality of the love-principle. The
Ascension of Christ is a space–time description of the universal
character of love. If this is not already clear in the Resurrection,
then it can be made clear in our celebration of Ascension.

The second note is the recognition of the presence of "heaven"
on earth. Rather than emphasizing the distance, the gap, between
heaven (understood as the locus of God) and earth (the abode of
men), the Ascension is actually an attempt to communicate their
inseparability since the Resurrection. Luther understood this
well. In his understanding, heaven is where God is. But, where
is God? The answer is, in the word and the sacraments—in short,
in the community which bears his name. The Ascension is a festi-

val to demonstrate God's presence through Christ in the world of men, a presence which does not abandon the world, but infuses it with meaning.

The third note is related to the second. It is the continuity of the Christian community through history, whether living or dead. The older theologians spoke of the church militant and the church triumphant, by which they meant the church on earth and the church in heaven. If heaven and earth are inseparable, then we need to recapture the thread of a historical continuum. It is in the Eucharist that this historical continuum is affirmed, especially in the preface where we are encouraged to see ourselves symbolically as being present with all the saints of the past before the "throne of God." The *unity* of the church in death and life is celebrated by the Ascension.

Ascension is the "bridge" in the tracking of experience between the truth of the Resurrection and the truth of the Pentecost season, which immediately follows it. Ascension is the "explosion of consciousness," by which the pieces of the unity of mankind come together clearly and the gap between life and death is overcome on a communal as well as an individual level. All of history is seen as consummated and fulfilled in the Easter-event through the added dimension of the Ascension. It leads into the season of the Spirit.

There is a fourth and final note on the meaning of the Ascension which ties the other three together from a theological point of view. It is that Ascension marks the entrance of Jesus into his *Kyrios*-ship. Jesus is Lord! This is the proclamation which is sealed by the "testimony" of the Ascension. This is clear from the texts for Exaudi, the Sunday after Ascension (because the Ascension texts are the record of the "event" itself). The Gospel (John 15:26 ff.) resounds the promise of the Spirit, who comes in the time of the *Kyrios*-ship of Christ. The Epistle (1 Peter 4:7 ff.) exhorts us to the universality of love and the exercise of our gifts in the Spirit, and leads up to a doxological conclusion in which we are reminded that "to [Jesus Christ] belong glory and dominion for ever and ever. Amen" (v. 11). With the Ascension, we perceive the cosmic dimensions of Christ, and his position as *Kyrios*,

as Lord of our lives. The coming season of the Spirit will expli-
cate this further, and the final season of the year, Advent, will
again return to the *Kyrios Jesous* from the perspective of the
future Parousia. With the Ascension, the critical consciousness of
the church and the place of the individual Christian "in, but not
of, the world" begins to dawn with increasing clarity.

THE NEW LIFE MEAL
(Easter)

Easter is the center of the church's revolutionary year, as it is
the center for a Christian life-style. Easter is the mystery which
designates the peculiarly Christian interpretation of reality; it is
the wisdom of God which opposes the foolishness of men. "Wisdom" here does not mean logic or rational speculation; it means
the radical breakthrough of the meaning of God in the center of
history, which is apprehended more by intuition than by investigation. Easter is the mystery that life is stronger than death, that
God's love is more pervasive than man's inhumanity. Easter, by
the radical proclamation and celebration of life, marks the death
of death, the dismantling of the power of death—beginning with
individual hearts and working its way through a community of
the Resurrection to all men. In the celebration of Easter, the
Christian proclaims his radical freedom from all the systems of
manipulation, exploitation, and death which the tyrannies of
men construct; he proclaims his allegiance to a higher power,
to the Risen Christ, whom we receive in word and sacrament
and whose presence we celebrate in community.

OPENING SONGS
OPENING VERSICLES
    V. Christ is risen. Christ is risen!
    R. He is risen in truth. Alleluia!
    V. Celebrate the banquet of the King.
    R. Celebrate the unity of mankind.
    V. Celebrate the death of death as power.

R. Celebrate the gifts of life and love.

V. Christ has broken the bars of death.

R. He has opened the prison and given new life to the captives.

V. The future lies open before us.

R. Its shape is love; therefore, we have hope.

THE STATEMENT OF PURPOSE

THE PSALM

THE FREE PRAYER *(Community response: "For Christ gives new life.")*

READINGS *(Other readings first; biblical readings last.)*

THE CONTEMPORARY WORD

THE AFFIRMATION

> Christ is risen, risen in truth.
> Here we celebrate the mystery
> that is denied abroad in the world.
> In our actions toward one another,
> we see the Christ living anew.
> His presence liberates us
> from all the fears of dying:
> Dying on the physical level,
> because he offers us life-with-God.
> Dying on the emotional level,
> slowly, by not growing to full manhood.
> Dying through all the many ways
> that we close off our lives to love.
> Within the community of the resurrection,
> a new society rises constantly, daily,
> on the ashes of broken dreams,
> on the pile of shattered ideologies,
> on the death-wagon of all systems.
> We are an outpost of the New World,
> a colony of peace and love and hope
> living side-by-side with the worlds
> of hatred and death and manipulation,
> breaking open the old worlds where we can.
> We seek the Spirit of Christ

who brings us to new life.

He is among us, in our meal,

and in our acts of love to one another.

Christ is risen, risen in truth!

MORE SONGS

THE OFFERING PERIOD (*Pick out your self-offering for the coming week—something you will do or not do—and reflect on it. Ask yourself how you can give yourself to share the meaning of new life with others.*)

THE EXTENSION OF THE COMMUNITY

1. *announcement of any coming events*
2. *statement of purpose for the next celebration*
3. *introduction of newcomers to the community*

SONG BEFORE THE COMMUNION LITURGY (*optional*)

THE NEW LIFE MEAL

THE RECONCILIATION PERIOD (*Face-to-face discussion, etc.*)

THE KISS OF PEACE

V. Christ is risen.

R. Christ is risen in truth!

THE SONG BEFORE THE MEAL (*optional*)

THE THANKSGIVING PRAYER

We give thanks to you, O God, for the creation in which we find ourselves. Our thanks arise for your creative power, which sustains our moment-by-moment existence and makes it more than mere existence. We thank you for our life, as the fruits of your creative power. By it we are united with all men through our creatureliness.

We praise you especially for the gift of Jesus, whom we call the Christ and Lord, by whose cross and resurrection new life is brought into the world. By his death he destroyed death and by his resurrection he opened the joys of life to all men. Through him we see life raised above the power of death, love exalted above hatred, and we see the guarantee for these in his rising again, the first fruits of new life in which we participate as we join in that meal he celebrated on the night of his betrayal, when he took bread, and when he had given thanks he broke it and gave it to his friends, saying, "Take and eat: this is my body which is given for you. In similar fashion he took the cup and, when he had drunk from it, he blessed it and gave it to them, saying, "Take this and drink it all of you: this cup is the new covenant in my blood, which is shed for you and for many for the forgiveness of sins. Do this often in memory of me."

We seek your Spirit, to bless both the bread and wine we offer here and to bless us by calling us to community, a community in which the Truth is not only affirmed but practiced. All honor and praise to you, O God whom we call our Father, for bringing us to new life through our Liberator, Jesus the Christ. Amen.

THE OUR FATHER

V. As often as we eat this bread and drink this cup:
R. We show forth the Lord's death until he comes.
V. Celebrate the mystery of the resurrection.
R. Let the community of love be built out from us.

THE NEW LIFE MEAL

TIME FOR SILENT REFLECTION *(How can the community of love be projected into the future beginning with this community, of which I am a member?)*

THE CLOSING THANKSGIVING PRAYER *(By a member.)*
CLOSING SONGS
THE BLESSINGS

V. Shall we thank the Lord once more?
R. Yes, we'll bless him once again.
V. Thanks be to God.
R. Thanks be to God, who gives us the victory!
V. Go forth with a renewed life.
Live out the joy of the resurrection.
Create the community of love where and
when you can.
Deepen your sense of unity with all mankind.
In the name and for the sake of Christ.
R. So be it! So shall we live!

TRUST

All true community is based on trust
  in the development of which
  we learn to be human
    truly human
    fully human to one another
at the center of which we simultaneously
      learn to see God.
Your trust in me is in proportion
  to my trust in you
  and it takes just a spark
     just a flash of light
       to open the door to a
       trusting relationship.
And the spark and the light are in the world
  but the world knows them not
  because the world is hung on the hook
     of its false standards of acceptance
     which are a roadblock
     before the doorway of trust.
When the light dawns
  when I see myself in the light
       in the gentle rays of the sun
         the Son
   at the point of my acceptance
     I am free
  to move out from myself
        . . . and trust.
Whenever one individual
    sees himself in the light
    he is the platform
    on which community can be built.
And there has been such an Individual
  and he gives power to other individuals
  who, seeing themselves in that same light,
  create the community of trust
        where they can
        where they are.

6

PENTECOST:

COMMUNITY IN THE SPIRIT

Pentecost is the season of deep spiritual experience. It is the season in which the church tries, through its liturgical thrust, to communicate the deepest levels of reality as apprehended through Christianity. These levels of reality are tied in with the revelation, begun in Incarnation and consummated in Resurrection, of the presence of God; everyday life is the proper domain of God. Grace is purveyed through nature. This is such a profound truth that it is almost impossible to communicate it without distortion. This is the season in which we see that love is the fulfilling of the law and that love is the law's replacement as *modus vivendi* for the Christian. As Augustine said, "Love God and do whatever you please." But this is hard to comprehend if God is not the source of reality which forms the construct for your whole life-style. It is easy enough to *say* that anyone who properly loves God will automatically live in a proper relation to nature and his fellowman; it is harder actually to do it. Love is so easily twisted into manipulation, patronization, and exploitation that it must be communicated carefully. This is the first reason we see for the high parable content in the Pentecost-season Gospels.

Parables are so obvious that they are obscure to those who do not have the "ears to hear"; their very simplicity is a mask, for the profundity of God is dreadfully simple. Holiness is simple in its engulfment of man; awe and wonder overcome you if you don't watch out. You must work to evade the presence of God. And men do work at it! To evade the presence of God, they go to great lengths, beginning with the intellectual suspension of "belief" in God.

The second reason the parabolic content is so high in the Pentecost season has to do with the *nature* of parables. A parable is a picture Jesus used to indicate the presence of God in the ordinary events of life and processes of nature. The meaning of the parables is not found by analogy but on the deepest level of spiritual experience: God is *in* the ordinary, he is not *like* the ordinary. But this is not a normal perception. To see the kingdom of God breaking into the world of ordinary events goes contrary to the mind of man, for man wishes—at all costs—to separate nature from grace so that he can compartmentalize his life to make it manipulable. The kingdom's presence means that God is among us; nature and grace are united. God's presence was announced in the Incarnation (Christ-mass), expanded by the Resurrection (Easter); and now the purpose of the Spirit (Pentecost and its season) is to indicate the presence of God in all of life, including interpersonal relationships. The Spirit leads us into all the truth, and the truth is that God is present . . . if we have the "ears to hear" and the "eyes to see."

Pentecost is simultaneously the season of communication. The relationship between community and communication is shown, first of all, in the imagery of the original Pentecost texts. The disciples—now become apostles through the Resurrection—communicate with men in other languages. It is the Tower of Babel (Genesis 11) tape run backward; man no longer strives to be like God, because the truth is that God has entered the mainstream of humanity. Community is established among men; our pride is unmasked as the force which disintegrates community. Communication, in the sense of the ability to share oneself with another in a way that will not divide but rather unify mankind, is now the norm among men; we proclaim it as a reality, in Christ, not as an ideal or a potential. It exists and we enter into it. The Pentecost season is the time of the revolutionary year for celebrating communication among men through the gifts of the Spirit.

During the Pentecost season we are forced again to look at the shape of our relationships with others, the assumption of the season being that one has had the experience of grace which underlies the ethical (as opposed to the moral, or "good") life. This emphasis on our relationships with others further demonstrates Pentecost as the season of the community. The Spirit builds community among men and this community is visible in the apprehension of the meaning of God within experience and demonstrated in the Resurrection of Christ (reason and revelation going together to form the whole).

The Easter season proclaimed the foundation for community in the Resurrection. The Pentecost season logically follows as the season for the building of community. It is the time of the peace of God which Jesus proclaims. It is the time of shalom, which is wholeness-in-community.

The other side of the matter is that Pentecost is the season when our religious insight begins to run out and it becomes increasingly clear how much we are dependent on God. We see the world around us and it is not hard to realize that the community the Spirit creates is not present among all men. If anything, the affairs of men and nations seem to run in the opposite direction to the community of mankind proclaimed in the Resurrection and created by the Spirit's gathering power.

Hence it is quite clear that the spiritual unity of mankind has not yet arrived. The kingdom has not come completely. So there must be a focus on the future. The community of faith is a community that lives in hope for the end when all things will be consummated and we will see clearly the divine nature within the whole creation. It is toward this end that the Spirit leads us, for this *is* the truth.

For individuals, it is possible to perceive the Spirit of unity so that they transcend time in their own experience, and all history is suddenly filled with cosmic significance. But the experience does not remain forever. The mount of Transfiguration must be left behind. Collectively, the church bears—in its celebration and proclamation—the truth of the Holy Spirit's mediation between God and man, the reestablishment of communication among men, the creation of the new human community. But these are ideals and not of the essence of reality to most people; the church bears this truth, is charged with this truth, even when it imperfectly realizes it.

The Spirit is the Spirit of freedom. His gifts are inspiration, enthusiasm, beauty, creativity, community. All are gifts which cannot be analyzed by rational models; they do not fit the scientific model of the universe as a related, logical system. Science rests on the *Logos*, but these aspects of life rest on the *Spirit*—which is one reason why words break apart when we try to communicate the experience of the Spirit. So, for centuries, the church has believed the Spirit more by hope than by realization, more as an expectation than as a datum of experience. We track the Spirit where we can, but like the wind he blows where he wills. "The Kingdom of God is righteousness and peace and joy (given by) the Holy Spirit" (Rom. 14:17). As the kingdom is futuristic in the gospel, so the Spirit is futuristic in the life of the church. We celebrate as much knowledge of the Spirit as we have.

And we celebrate this knowledge in a community. The kingdom remains a community, and it is the communal meaning of the Spirit which is emphasized in the long Pentecost season. By our apprehension of the divine-human nature of creation, a divine-human community is built, however tenuous it may appear, in which the gifts of the Spirit manifest themselves, and in which men are thereby led to wholeness. The Pentecost season is the time for the actualization of shalom.

In less theological terms, the Pentecost season corresponds to man's search for a construct of meaning and wholeness by which to organize his life. It matches our experience of dis-integration and lack of communion with others and holds out the possibility of wholeness as it is experienced in the divine-human community. Pentecost is the time of demonstration of the Christian way of life, which accepts all things and people as a gracious gift of

God and hence avoids building the mental walls of separation, the things we call defense mechanisms. Defense mechanisms are necessary when the ego is unstable; once you realize your essential unity with others in an I-Thou relationship, however, you can throw them away. The Pentecost season matches the process by which men overcome their selfishness, their egocentricity, and open up to others.

This "opening up" comes in bits and pieces; it is not total. It is made with people you trust, with whom you can be "personal" because they respect your person. It comes with people with whom you create a community. This is the link between the church's teaching of the Spirit and the experience of the individual; wherever a true community is found—the attributes of which are love, trust, concern, and honesty—there the Spirit is operative.

The Pentecost season is a season of tension: the tension is that between the "already" of the life in the Spirit because of the Resurrection, and the "not yet" of the end, the consummation of all things in Christ. The community of faith, with its imperfectly realized love and trust, feels this tension but nevertheless moves toward the eschaton by virtue of its faith and obedience. There is a high ethical content in the Gospels that are read during the Pentecost season. It is an ethical content for Christians, for those whose value system is being shaped by the Resurrection of Christ. It is an ethical content for those who have made a commitment to the centrality of the Resurrection as a determinative force for their life-style. The key concepts for the ethic of the Christian are the gifts of the Spirit: love, peace, joy, hope, and faith. These concepts are of far greater significance than the ethic because they are based on the Resurrection, which is the center for all Christian faith and life.

The purpose of the Pentecost season is to point to the many functions of the Holy Spirit. We have suggested two possible purposes beyond this in the parabolic nature of reality as shown in some of the Gospels, and in the ethic of the Resurrection based on faith and obedience which is worked out in the community. The gifts of the Spirit are the means by which both of these purposes are given life in the church. Their use, their continuous upbuilding in the church, is the means by which the community is built.

A final function of the Spirit is twofold: on the one hand, to mediate the presence of Christ, and on the other hand, to draw up and undergird man's experience of Christ. So the meaning of the Spirit for the church is quite clear: it is he who consummates our knowledge of God-in-Christ and thereby leads us into all the truth, providing the means whereby the community of shalom is built in the world of man, as a sort of human arrow pointing beyond itself to the consummation of all the world at the end. The Spirit is both with us and ahead of us, for the community never fully actualizes the reality of human unification given in the Resurrection. Man remains, as Luther said, *simul justus et peccator*. He cannot create utopia, because utopia is literally "nowhere." But he can participate in the reality of unity within the comunity which the Spirit gathers.

This leads us to one final practical consideration: the Pentecost season is the time for looking more clearly than before at the cultural nexus in which we live. Liturgically the season should prepare us for hard, objective looking at the culture in which we find ourselves, armed for such scrutiny by the knowledge of what the human community *could* be. We look at the culture on the basis of our faith and the consciousness that faith produces. This consciousness stands against the manipulative culture. It stands against it on several levels, the most austere and shaking of which is our commitment as Christians to an absolute in the universe, whom we call God.

As the Spirit leads us more deeply into the truth, we sense the further tension between our faith and the life of the world. If there is primary tension between the end and the now in Christianity, there is secondary tension between the world and the faith. The more deeply we enter into the truth of the Spirit, the more sharply do we feel the pinch of the world. As we live in and of the Spirit, we are forced to the classic Christian position of living in, but not of, the world. We are led to a position where we see the yawning gap between what is and what ought to be.

The world of God breaks into the world of men and we experience it in part, but never as a whole, yet we celebrate the wholeness, the shalom, in which we participate. This has tremendous implications for the Christian community.

The modern world founds its value systems apart from absolutes; there is no ought-ness in the world. The materials are simply not there to build any sense of ought-ness. Christianity proclaims a vision of a world that ought-to-be, but this very proclamation is suspect from the world's point of view, because the world does not have the absolutes necessary to construct any imperatives for the future or the present. The world is thus reduced to either possibility or necessity in shaping values. Repression becomes necessary to control society, hence it is put into the value system of the leadership class. Biogenetic engineering is possible, so it becomes part of the value system. Man, reduced to the position of either an animal or a machine, is manipulable because he is definable in terms that not only declare him capable of manipulation but which indicate that —with the right form of engineering—he can be altered into anything that someone with more power wants to alter him to. There is no respect for the individual in such a system; individual man's dignity is given him, not by God by virtue of his being made in the image of God, but rather by man and whatever man wants to shape his fellowman into. Christianity stands *opposed* to this understanding of man reduced to biological terms and technological possibility. The season of Pentecost turns us over to an absolute power from which we derive the perspective necessary to criticize the world in which we live.

Pentecost is thus the time for a sharpening of consciousness from a perspective of faith. It is a time for the upbuilding of the community with the gifts of the Spirit: love, peace, joy, faith, and hope. Not that the whole year is not the time for this, but the Pentecost season draws our attention to it in a crucial way. It is the season for model-building for the future, in the light of our insights into the meaning of the kingdom of God. The inability of Christianity to create exciting models of the future, other than the old tired repetition of biblical symbols, is a judgment on our inability to grasp both the complex content of the Spirit's work in the world, and at the same time a condemnation of our willingness to accept uncritically the models the world offers us, most of which are based at worst on a value system with no base in absolutes of any kind and at best on a' humanistic technology which still leaves open the question of the origin of manipulation. Pentecost is the season of fantasy within the church. The future is fantasized in this season, based on the Resurrection and the presence of Christ through the Spirit, based on the individual life-style which is shaped by peace, joy, hope, love, and faith, based on the cosmic nature of the community and the communication patterns which are celebrated in Christianity.

THE SHALOM MEAL
(Pentecost)

Shalom is the biblical concept for the realities of wholeness, peace, justice, and reconciliation. For individuals, it means the ability to reach your human potential, which comes from acceptance, love, and affirmation by God and your fellowman. For two people, it may mean the ability to reconcile differences and come to a new understanding of one another. For communities, it means an affirmative style of life for all in the community, in which they are encouraged and outfitted to reach their potential. On the broad plane of society and government, it means justice. In every relationship, it carries the dominant overtone of peace. The Community of the Spirit lives by the concept of shalom, attempting to open up the reality that is shalom in everything we do. In the season of the Spirit (Pentecost), we celebrate the reality the Spirit brings: shalom-in-community. The Shalom Meal is a community celebration to assist in the realization of shalom.

OPENING SONGS
OPENING VERSICLES
     V. Glory to God in the highest:
     R. And peace to men in whom God is pleased.

V. Peace be upon this house.

R. And to all who dwell herein.

V. Those who work for peace are happy.

R. God will call them his sons.

V. Live in peace,

R. And the God of love and peace will be with you.

V. The peace of the Lord be with you.

R. And with you, too.

THE STATEMENT OF PURPOSE

THE PSALM

THE FREE PRAYER *(Community response:* "We seek the peace of God.")

READINGS *(Other readings first; biblical readings last.)*

THE CONTEMPORARY WORD

THE AFFIRMATION

We believe in God.

God is shalom.

Shalom is justice and equity.

Shalom is peace and love.

Shalom is reconciliation and wholeness.

Shalom is community and deep relationships.

God is found in these realities

wherever they may happen.

God is found in our community

as we live these realities.

Jesus is the bringer of shalom,

who announces it anew and lives for it.

He has, by his cross, enabled us

to accept ourselves (as God accepts us)

so that we may live shalom

toward our fellowman.

His resurrection indicates

the shape of shalom for all men.

The Spirit creates from us

the community of shalom.

Living or dead we are in God.

Living or dead we are in shalom.

We are free to live, free to die.
Let us live in shalom.

MORE SONGS

THE OFFERING PERIOD (*Here, individuals in the community are asked to pick out something they will do or not do for the coming week and offer themselves in the task.*)

THE EXTENSION OF THE COMMUNITY
1. *announcement of any coming events*
2. *statement of purpose for the next celebration*
3. *introduction of newcomers to the community*

SONG BEFORE THE COMMUNION LITURGY *(optional)*

THE SHALOM MEAL

THE RECONCILIATION PERIOD (*Here, individuals are asked to enter into a face-to-face relationship . . . etc.*)

THE KISS OF PEACE

V. Salute one another with a holy kiss.

R. Christ is in the midst of us!

THE SONG BEFORE THE MEAL *(optional)*

THE THANKSGIVING PRAYER

God of wholeness and reconciliation, we call upon you in thanksgiving for our life and the life of the world around us, for song and dance, for tree and flower, for city and country. At the same time we call upon you in sadness, seeking new awareness of the fragmented and broken world in which we live, new ways of demonstrating your presence in it for the world to see the new human society of shalom.

Jesus, our brother and lord, created that new society and, to celebrate it, gathered his community as we gather ours, breaking bread and sharing wine with the words, "This is my body, broken for you" and "This is my blood, poured out for you. Do this in memory of me."

Only the Spirit creates the community of love and wholeness, for only he gathers men into the truth. We seek his presence. Be with us now, O Creator Spirit, by whose word we are gathered together in the community of love and trust which is the island of faith in a blinded world. To the almighty God be power and glory forever and ever. Amen.

THE OUR FATHER

THE SHALOM MEAL

FANTASY PERIOD FOR SHARING AND BUILDING THE COMMUNITY *(Here, in the free flow of words and feelings, we try as individuals and as a community to fantasize new life-styles for ourselves and for the community as a whole, seeking ways to bring shalom to others and seeking ways to bring others to shalom. Nonverbal expressions are invited.)*

CLOSING SONGS

THE BLESSINGS

    V. Go in peace. Go in love.

       Share the community of shalom.

       Deepen your relationships with all men.

       In the name and for the sake of Christ.

    R. So be it. So shall we live.

CENTERING DOWN

At the very center of life
   there stands bedrock of mystery;
Granite,
   immovable, yet good;
Call it humanity.

No drill so sharp to penetrate
   the complex at the core of life;
No words so smooth to inundate
   the well-plowed fields of mind and heart.

In times of stillness and of noise,
   in times when others chatter round,
We catch a glimpse of mystery
   that comes
   when we're centering down.

Then comes the knifelike shaft of light
   that burns our eyes,
   redeems our soul;
Ourselves we see beyond the night
   where we know we're whole.

7

ADVENT:

THE COMING OF THE LORD

The Advent season is built upon the resurrection hope and the proleptic community of the Spirit. It draws the revolutionary year to a close, because it projects the Parousia, the "Second Coming of Christ" as a panoramic vista under which all history and all existence and all experience stand. The confusing celebration of Christ-mass within this season is a practical problem that effectively overshadows it and has tended, historically, to rob it of its drama and proclamatory power. The season stands in its own right, however, and needs to be raised up as a separate entity, unconnected with Christ-mass in the way it is normally connected (e.g., the Fourth Sunday in Advent is celebrated as Christ-mass Sunday in many churches, which robs us of the opportunity to hear the final Advent message of preparation for the *future*. Although the Christ-mass season bears within it the seeds for celebrating the coming of Christ "to the hearts of men now," this confusion blurs the distinction even further between history, experience of the individual, and the Parousia, all of which are distinct elements in the liturgical process of consciousness-raising).

Advent is the season of the *Kyrios*. Through the Resurrection Jesus is demonstrated as Lord by the power of God, and in the

season of the Spirit he is experienced in community and the
gathering reunification of man. During Advent Jesus as *Kyrios* is
seen within the framework of the eschatological drama of fulfillment for the universe which is symbolized as the Parousia, the
"second coming," the "end of the ages," the dissolution of the
"heavens and the earth" in a *new* heaven and a *new* earth, celebrated in the last book of the Bible, Revelation (chapter 20).

The concept of Jesus as *Kyrios* means primarily three things:

(1) He is given the equivalence of divinity through the Resurrection. Now we see him in his participation in the God whom he
proclaimed as "Our Father." Because of this, the words of Gregory
Nazianzus begin to make more sense: "God became man in order
that man might become God." The *Kyrios*-ship of Jesus is the
model for the Christian eschatological vision of man. In Christ
and in the Body of Christ which is the liturgical community, we
participate in the "divinization" of man. Man moves toward his
fulfillment in the pattern of Christ. The implications for a life-
style are drawn out in the fact that our Lord is simultaneously
the Suffering Servant. We participate in his passion as the world
moves toward the Eschaton (Col. 1:24; 2 Cor. 1:5), in the collective Body of Christ suffering toward the completion of man's
destiny.

(2) Jesus has our highest allegiance. The political dimensions
of the recognition of the *Kyrios*-nature of Jesus are clear. Obedience to him as our "Caesar" puts us in a position of living in, but
not of, the systems of the world. From this position, criticism of
the culture, rather than a placid and powerless acceptance of
its power over life, is possible. The manipulation and exploitation
of man are unmasked. Baptism as *sacramentum* is related to the
lordship of Christ. The *sacramentum* was the Roman soldier's
oath of allegiance given to demonstrate his loyalty unto death to
Caesar. Baptism is thus our oath of allegiance to the *Kyrios
Christos*, the oath of allegiance to the one who simultaneously
frees us from the death-process of the world and its systems and
enables us to adopt the critical attitude from which to work in
and for the world. All earthly allegiances—family, culture, world,
system of government, political ideology—are put into perspec-

tive as wholly secondary and imperfect in the light of the *Kyrios*-nature of Christ. Our allegiance to the *Kyrios Christos* is the declaration of our freedom. In obedience to him we find the radical freedom which caused Luther to marvel at the paradox of the Christian style: "The Christian is a perfectly free lord of all, subject to none. The Christian is a perfectly dutiful servant of all, subject to all" (*Treatise on Christian Liberty*).

(3) Jesus as *Kyrios* is mediator of a perfected union of man with God (1 Tim. 2:5; 1 John 2:1), which has yet to be fully realized but which is a gift, and not a task for man to work for. The cross is interpreted by the Resurrection (as the riddle deserves an answer) and the Resurrection is further interpreted by the confession, "Jesus is Lord" (the primitive confession of the church; see 1 Cor. 1:10; Rom. 10:9 f.; Phil. 2:5–11; Acts 2:36; 4:33 *inter alia*). Now Jesus is the mediator through whom all men are given communion with God—a new relationship of love and forgiveness, overcoming the alienation of the world. We participate in this life because of the cross and Resurrection, and in the Advent season we celebrate the triumph of the new life in miniscule, looking toward the eschatological completion of the Parousia.

The Advent season is the season in which the religious experience of man runs out completely in the inbreaking of God's divine order. There is no experience to correlate with the truth the Advent season bears. While it is possible to sketch existential similarities between the life of the individual and the data of the historical faith in the other seasons, these similarities come to an end in Advent. Whereas the Christ-mass, Lenten, and Easter seasons correlate with man's experience of the divine within life (however dimly perceived, at times), Pentecost forms a bridge from those times to the still higher truth and carries with it the community of faith as well as is able. But this bridge breaks down in Advent. God speaks; we listen. Perhaps because of the fact that we cannot comprehend the futuristic truth of this season any further, we end the year with the Advent season. There seem to be two logical reasons for ending the revolutionary year with Advent:

(1) It is the season for contemplating the highest/deepest truth which is to be found. The Advent season is the end of our experience.

(2) It is the church's representation of the end and its call to Christians to expect the end. So there is nowhere to go but to begin the cycle anew at Christ-mass.

The whole Advent season is dependent solely on the action of God; therefore there is no recourse but to return to the beginning again and repeat the cycle from Christ-mass on. Hence Advent takes on the character of the season of *expectation* and *waiting*. The season is for reflection on the meaning of our expectation and our waiting, which are undergirded by hope in the coming Christ. We have experienced the hope-ful nature of the universe, the cosmos emerging from chaos in the Incarnation, Resurrection, and the season of the Spirit. Now we use the time of Advent to sound the note of *hope* in the midst of a nihilistic world, a world bent on death and destruction.

There are two links between the Parousia which the season celebrates and the present. The first is, of course, the historical link which is sounded in the Gospels of the season (which we will look at in detail a little further on). The older scholarly theory of *Urzeit/Endzeit* plays its part in the symbolism of the season. As the beginning of the experience of God-in-Christ, so shall the end be—only both qualitatively and quantitatively more. *Quantitatively* more because it embraces the universe (Rom. 8: 18–25 celebrates this). *Qualitatively* more because it means the transformation of the universe (Revelation 20–21). Yet the end is like the beginning, as the full-grown ear of corn is like the seed; in other words, it is the actualization of that which is already potentially unfolding in the love, joy, peace, hope, and faith of the present community. The historical texts are symbolic projections of the future based on the data of experience in the community of faith. This gives us a clue as to the projections of the present community. The Christian community has shown itself remarkably unimaginative and unexciting in its projection of the future; one wonders why this is so, because at least the materials we need in terms of attitudes, concepts, world view, and so on are already within the gospel message itself. The Advent season is the time for us to "remember the future."

The second link between the Parousia and the present is in the liturgical pattern of word and sacrament of the gathered community. As the pattern is a demonstration of the Christian life-style, so it is also a demonstration of the coming fulfilled relationships within the universe. Our celebration is itself an anticipation of the messianic banquet, the supper of the Great King, at the end of time and a demonstration of our expectation of the fulfillment of time at the Parousia of Christ. At this meal, no differences among men matter. Rich and poor, male and female, black and white—these distinctions have no significance, except perhaps to remind us of the *in*equality we blasphemously perpetuate among men which frustrates the purposes of the kingdom of God. The differences our minds create that block our perception of the unification of mankind in Christ are overcome in our celebration.

Because Advent is so obscured in the revolutionary year, we wish to spend some time in this chapter in a consideration of the texts for the season as a means of recovering its nature as the season of the *Kyrios Christos*.

The *collects* for the season are consistent in their thrust. They sound three notes throughout the season:

(1) The confident expectation of the church that the Lord will come. The church fully expects the consummation promised in the gospel at the end of time.

(2) The recognition that we live "between the times," i.e., between the time of the Resurrection and the time of the Eschaton. This recognition brings to the community a certain consciousness of its unique place in the life of the world.

(3) The recognition that the matter is out of our hands, that the consummation cannot be produced by the action of man, but that our sin constantly obscures the final fulfillment of man. In conjunction with this, there is renewed calling upon the *Kyrios* to present himself so that the alienation of man might finally be overcome, but never from the viewpoint that we can do it of our own volition or power.

The pericopes for the season further enhance the expectant nature of the season:

The Gospel for Advent I (Matt. 21:1–9) may be seen as a proleptic projection of the past event of Christ's entry into Jerusalem as a metaphor for his "entrance" at the end of time. The Epistle undergirds this with its note that "salvation is nearer to us now than when we first believed" (Rom: 13:12) and by exhorting us to "put on the *Kyrios Jesous Christos*" (v. 14). We expect the entrance of a king, one whom we serve in ultimate allegiance now, but whose kingship has yet to be understood within the totality of creation.

The Gospel for Advent II is from the "little apocalypse" of Luke 21 and parallels, which is clearly a fantasy of the future, pointing out the strife between good and evil (overcome in Christ), and climaxing with the promise: "heaven and earth will pass away [i.e., it is in the nature of God that present reality be drawn up and consummated into a new thing], but my words will not pass away." The comfort of this promise is part of the hope-construct of the season. The Epistle underwrites the hope-filledness of this coming consummation with its prayer that "by the Power of the Spirit you may abound in hope" (Rom. 15:13). Again we are reminded that the shape of the cosmos is not a threat to man, but is "friendly." God-is-love has come in the cross and Resurrection, and this is a constant truth throughout history which the Christian community celebrates, a truth man is not ready to accept, but which is breaking in and will break in conclusively at the end of time.

The Gospel for Advent III (Matt. 11:2–10) may be viewed in two ways. It can be seen either as a liturgical transference of the messenger status of John to the church which bears the embryo of the coming kingdom, or as an indication that the works of love demonstrated as part of the Messiah-nature of Jesus are now carried on in the church. Either way it points to the community as bearer of the reality which the world does not comprehend, but which will be fulfilled at the end. In the action of the community, Christ is at work, but his final act is yet to come. The Epistle seems to corroborate such an understanding with its note that we of the church are "servants of Christ and stewards of the mysteries of God," awaiting the time when "the Lord comes, who will bring to light the things now hidden in darkness and will disclose the purposes of the heart" (1 Cor. 4:1–5). This Sunday clearly points to the "sacramental" nature of the Christian community, as the bearer of the truth of the gospel in the midst of the world.

The Gospel for Advent IV sounds the note of the inbreaking Christ. The words of John, "among you stands one whom you do not know," are repeated to the church as a final reminder of the mysterious presence of Christ the Lord, a presence imperfectly recognized in the community, but nevertheless a presence of power. The Epistle (Phil. 4:4 ff.) reminds us of our *position* in the world and our *attitude* toward God: "Rejoice in the Lord always. . . . The Lord is at hand. Have no anxiety about anything. . . . And the peace of God, which passes all understanding, keep your hearts and minds in Christ Jesus."

We have been brought to the end, and so to a new beginning. The revolutionary year has completed its cycle, drawing up the experience of man into the history of God, correlating personal experience of the divine with the unfolding of God's purpose in the world, showing the divine-human nature of the world and of the community of Christ. Advent turns us back at the breaking point of consciousness to the original miracle in history, the miracle of the Incarnation. We return to Christ-mass to repeat the cycle again. Each time the cycle is repeated, there is a deepening consciousness of the meaning of God's act in Christ for all of life. The revolutionary year gives us a ground upon which to organize our subjective experience. Centering on the Resurrection, it helps us to work backward from there to the historic root of the Christian faith in the birth of Jesus and forward to the consummation of creation at the Eschaton. Slowly, over a period of years, the church's revolutionary year builds our faith, raises our consciousness, and gives us the handles we are looking for to interpret our own experience and intimations of the divine in the midst of life.

THE MARANATHA MEAL
(Advent)

Maranatha! was the victory cry of early Christians. It means "Our Lord, come!" (Rev. 22:20b; 1 Cor. 16:22b). It may also have the overtone of "Our Lord is the sign—Alpha and Omega." It was a watchword of hope and encouragement; and an early second-century writing called the Didache uses it in a eucharistic prayer. To say "Our Lord, come" *means* to grow and work toward peace and justice, in the hope that God's peace and fulfillment will eventually fill all creation. It is the mystery of our liturgy to celebrate the total presence of Christ in our midst . . . here . . . tonight . . . to give us a glimpse of the radical future.

OPENING SONGS
OPENING VERSICLES
    V. Everything is ready. Come to the wedding feast.
    R. Many are invited, but few are chosen.
    V. God's plan, which he will complete at the right time, is to bring all creation together:
    R. Everything in heaven and on earth, with Christ as head.
    V. When the Lord Jesus comes with all who belong to him:
    R. We will be holy and perfect in the presence of God.
    V. The Day of the Lord will come like a thief in the night:
    R. We who are in the light will not be surprised.
    V. Be patient, then, my brothers, until the Lord comes:
    R. We shall keep our hopes high!

THE STATEMENT OF PURPOSE
THE PSALM
THE FREE PRAYER (*Community response:* "Come, Lord Jesus, with your life-giving power!")
READINGS (*Other readings first; biblical readings last.*)
THE CONTEMPORARY WORD
THE AFFIRMATION

        Into the midst of a broken life
        and a frightened humanity
        and a confusing world
        comes the Christ, bearing gifts:

forgiveness for past hurts,
joyful new life, and
wholeness for man and his world.
We celebrate these gifts
as we celebrate his presence.
He comes among us gathered here,
and this is not by our own doing.
Like the Emmaus Road disciples,
He comes into our midst in
the proclamation of the freeing Word,
the meal of our new human society,
and the love he builds in our community.
We are an outpost of the radical faith;
We demonstrate his presence,
celebrating for the whole world
the Truth it cannot yet celebrate.
Here we know in bits and pieces,
but we live in the hope that,
any day now, we shall know the Fullness.
Come, Lord Jesus, among us!
Come, Lord Jesus, when time runs out!

MORE SONGS

THE OFFERING PERIOD

THE EXTENSION OF THE COMMUNITY
1. *announcement of any coming events*
2. *statement of purpose for the next celebration*
3. *introduction of newcomers to the community*

SONG BEFORE THE COMMUNION LITURGY *(optional)*

THE MARANATHA MEAL

THE RECONCILIATION PERIOD *(Face-to-face discussion, etc.)*

R. As we deal with one another, so we feel the presence, the affirmation, and the forgiveness of God which is promised us.

THE KISS OF PEACE

V. Salute one another with a holy kiss.
R. Christ is in the midst of us.

THE SONG BEFORE THE MEAL *(optional)*

THE THANKSGIVING PRAYER

We give thanks to you, O God our Father, for the mystery of the world which you have entrusted us with in the form of a community of love and trust, the anti-system which opposes the dehumanizing systems of life men create. In this community, we learn to be with each other and through it we receive the power to give and receive love. The community is our life-giving well; it is a mystery more than our coming-together; in it we see the meaning of Christ and glimpse the fulfillment of mankind at the end-time when you will draw all things together in love and peace.

The meal which Jesus gave us is our foretaste of the heavenly banquet; in it we see the false divisions and distinctions between men break down and dissolve before our eyes and we see each other as we are, people to be loved and affirmed, not objects to be manipulated. To show us the path, our brother Jesus took the bread and the wine and gave thanks for them and gave them to all mankind as a token of the world that is coming into this world. He gave them to us as his body and blood, that we might become his Body in the world.

Send the Spirit of Truth and Power to gather us together as one in Christ; and unto you, O Father, be all glory forever. Amen.

THE OUR FATHER

    V. As often as you eat this bread and drink this cup:

    R. We show forth the Lord's death until he comes.

    V. Celebrate the mystery of Christ's presence:

    R. Come, Lord Jesus: be with us now!

THE MARANATHA MEAL

THE CLOSING THANKSGIVING PRAYER *(By a member of the community.)*

CLOSING SONGS

THE BLESSINGS

    V. Shall we thank the Lord once more?

    R. Yes, we'll bless him once again.

    V. Bless we the Lord.

R. Thanks be to God, who is with us tonight.

V. Go in peace. Go in love.
Watch and wait for the final fulfillment of man.
Until that time, celebrate community with others.
Deepen your relationships with all men.
In the name and for the sake of Christ.

R. So be it! So shall we live!

GIVEN THE OPTIONS . . .

I thought I could find God
in the depth of my mind
and in living the very best
of all ethical lives and
dying for all kinds of causes.
But it was not enough.

I thought I could find God
in the depth of experience
and in living the most authentic
of all possible lives and
dying, if need be, to prove myself.
But it was not enough.

I thought I could find God
in the depth of religion
and in living a life concocted
of many strains of religion
and dying to myself mystically.
But it was not enough.

I thought I could find God
in the depth of my body
and trying the most pleasurable
of all good lives and
dying with a smile on.
But it was not enough.

I never thought I could find God
in the cross and resurrection
and in living the most faithful
of all my lives in order to
die with no regrets about . . .
But I did; it's enough.

8

SAINTS' DAYS:

FATHERS OF THE REVOLUTION

The poets and the dreamers, the actors and the thinkers, the young and the old, those whose pens scribed millions of words and those who wrote nothing—they came to an experience that crushed their souls and expanded their minds, an experience that liberated their consciousness from the systems and institutions that bound them in. So they were free in a radical sense, free in a revolutionary sense, free in a way that put them in position to judge their cultures in the light of ends, ends determined by the Resurrection.

They carried their freedom with them, even into chains and death. They had been liberated from the power of death and the coercive death-force of all the systems of the world. They lived in, but not of, the world in most creative ways. They put their faith not in an idea, not in an alternative system, not in a political ideology, but in a breakthrough of reality which they recognized in a person and the community which was created about him.

These people are called Saints—with a capital "s"—to distinguish them from the total community of Christians, who are also called saints.

A saint is someone who is "holy" (*sanctus* is the Latin word). This is a word which has taken on bad connotations today. "Holiness" is equated with prudery, piety, and puritanism in the minds of many people. Better labels for what holiness is, in current language, would be "commitment," "soul," "charisma," "dedication," "integrity." Holiness in the case of the Saints of the church does not necessarily mean purity of life, as we would consider that today (in terms of middle-class morality and virtues). These peopel were possessed of a certain type of religious piety, however different that piety may have been in each person's life. But piety is also not the root of holiness. The Saints were recognized not because of their piety and their purity (both of which are relative terms, relative to where you see yourself), but because of their lives as a whole, lives which exhibited a quality of radical distinction from the world around them. They were people with a difference (even though that difference might be chiefly internal), men and women on a mission, people somehow set apart from the dehumanizing conditions within which they lived, from the systems that entrapped other men, from the false gods and religions of men's minds. Set apart = holy = Saint. The capital letter means that their Christian peers, brothers and sisters within the same historic community, living out the same reality, recognized in them a fuller penetration of the mystery, a fuller comprehension of the faith, a more deeply fulfilled/actualized life than in themselves. So they affirmed their "set-apart-ness" by capitalizing the word; which makes the distinction one of *quantity* and not of *quality*.

The Saints are the historical behavioral models of the church, but this is not to be understood in a surface way. They are meant to be seen as individuals who exhibited a life-style worthy of consideration, not for its characteristics so much as for its principles and its underlying attitude. Nobody ought to get involved in any cheap imitation of the Saints (though I suppose there is little danger of that) any more than one would get involved in a cheap imitation of Jesus; this is not the function of their days. The function of the Saints' Days is to raise before our eyes brothers and sisters of the past community of the faith who are worthy of consideration because of their faith, and the way it issued forth in a life-style.

This raises a point for the Protestant church, which has systematically destroyed the calendar of Saints between the Apostles and the Reformation, and ignored any additions since the Reformation. In celebrations at the Community of the Spirit, in addition to the days commemorating the apostles, we use other Saints' Days. We use Saints from the early church: Basil, the two Gregories, Anselm, John the Damascene, and so on. In addition we celebrate the days of Dietrich Bonhoeffer, Martin Luther King, and others of the modern world who valued the Christian style of life and consciously acted it out. In house-church liturgies within the cycle of the year it is possible to do this once again, and to offer more models for consideration. One might call this doing theology by reflecting on biography. The history of the Saints is brought down to current times; we celebrate the presence of the Saints through the union of church "triumphant" with church "militant" in the Eucharist. And, in very *ancient* style, those moderns who are considered as Saints are proposed out of the community itself, as examples of what the community sees as a viable and deep Christian life-style . . . which was how we got Saints in the first place.

Building on a platform of seeing the Saints as models for the saints of all ages who participate in the mystery of the Resurrection, then, there appear to be five useful purposes in celebrating Saints' Days:

1. The celebration of Saints' Days is a means of recollecting the historical continuity of the faith. When the Saints are approached through modern eyes, and their lives are interpreted in ways we can make contact with, they appear to be as vital now as ever; but beyond this, they serve to remind us that there is a historic continuity to the Christian faith, a sort of changeless quality about it—changeless because it rests on truth revealed in the Resurrection. Saints' Days serve not only to link us to the past, but also to indicate the eternal nature of the Christian community.

2. The celebration of Saints' Days is a means of holding up

before us examples of the Christian life-style as it has been lived in other ages. This is not so antiquarián an interest as it may at first appear to be; the Saints exhibit in their lives timeless qualities of peace, love, joy, hope, and faith acted out in concrete cultural situations. Insofar as their cultures remind us of our own, their life-style is an analogy for our own.

3. The celebration of Saints' Days is a means for strengthening contemporary faith. Frequently in celebrations, we will read portions of a Saint's writing, translated into modern English, then discuss it to see the depth of the faith in ancient times and how it correlates to the nature of the faith in the present. The Saints of old went through life with convictions that were not shaken by fear, coercion, imprisonment, sickness and death, and from them we learn that such a faith can be our own. They show the depth of relationship to God that is possible for all Christians.

4. The celebration of the Saints' Days is a means for the community to affirm the eternal validity of the Christian faith. By dipping back now and then into the past of the faith, it becomes clearer and clearer as time goes by that we are part of a "red thread of tradition" stretching back to the Resurrection. In addition to the confirmation of individual faith that is assisted through the celebration of the Saints' Days, there is also the affirmation of the collective communal faith of the centuries.

5. In a somewhat more mystical way, but still connected with points 3 and 4 above, the celebration of the Saints' Days offers us a means to plug into the whole community of Christ, both living and dead. In the Eucharist, we come together with these Saints of old in union through Christ. People seek various ways in which to come into contact with "the other side"—through mediums, seances, or other occult wonders. Either that, or they wind up concluding that the only thing they can do is plant roses on their departed husband's gravesite. Between these two extremes lies an understanding of the mystical union of all Christians, whether living or dead, in the eucharistic meal. I communicate with my long-deceased father as I communicate with the community in the Eucharist. I find this a source of com-

fort which is not sloppy sentimentalism or esoteric occult mystery, but something that lies within the purview of the historic catholic faith of the church. In connection with this, one of the practices of the Community of the Spirit is, on All Saints' Day, to stop in the midst of the eucharistic prayer at the remembrance of the Saints and to add all the names of deceased relatives, friends, models, that have been written down by the liturgical president before the liturgy begins. We simply ask people for names of the people they want specially commemorated within the liturgical pattern. Shocking though this may be from a "protestant" viewpoint, it offers dramatic links for those in the community and stands on long catholic tradition. It is an affirmation of one of the lines of one of our community hymns: "One is living, one is not: that's a role that we play." The Community transcends time at the eucharistic meal; we demonstrate this in our liturgical practice.

The Saints are the Fathers of the Revolution; in them, we see a penetration of the mystery of God in Christ that is worth considering. They are sacred for us, in just the same way that my father, my uncle Will, and a few other people who are dead, are sacred for me. Rather than put down that aspect of sacredness, in the eucharistic assembly we gather *all* together to celebrate those who have had special meaning for our lives. Think of the Saints' Days as being the church's collective memory of those who have had special meaning for its life, and the correlation is not far-fetched, but rather obvious. And so the Saints' Days, and particularly All Saints' Day, are a means of utilizing again our experience of the sacred in others, merging with the experience of the sacred in the historic Saints of the church.

FATHERS OF THE REVOLUTION
(Saints' Days)

We live in a historical milieu. In a large measure, it is within the power of each man to choose the historical past to which he adheres. Each of us is a storyteller; we can make up endless stories about who we are, where we have come from. All of them are true; they just reflect different facets of our personalities. For we are many identities. Within the Christian faith, there is a special thread of history, a story which is that of each man in the faith. It is the story of the community of the faith which has historical roots and present reality and which will have future validity and life-forming power. Within this community, there have been certain fools for Christ who have been considered exemplary in their life-style and faith. They were not super-human; they were real humans who reached more of their poten-tial than the average man. In this special liturgy we celebrate these real humans, the Fathers of the Revolution.

OPENING SONGS

OPENING VERSICLES
> V. We are all witnesses.
> R. We are witnesses to the truth that sets men free.
> V. Our history is lined with fools and beggars.
> R. Their lives pave our history with gold and silver.
> V. They are the mirrors of the power of Christ:
> R. They are the reflection of true humanity-in-community.
> V. Let us celebrate tonight again our history.
> R. Let us celebrate the Fathers of the Revolution.

THE STATEMENT OF PURPOSE (*Which Father is celebrated tonight.*)

THE PSALM

THE FREE PRAYER (*Community response:* "For the witness is peace and love.")

READINGS (*Other readings first; biblical readings last.*)

THE CONTEMPORARY WORD (*Usually a discussion of the life-style and writings of the Saint of the day.*)

THE AFFIRMATION
> Down the corridors of history
> Along the hallways of time
> They came dancing and singing
> They came praying and loving.
> They came with a song of freedom,

They came with the joy of community;
They came under the banner of Truth.
They are the poets and the dreamers,
the actors and thinkers, the young and old;
They are the Fathers of the Revolution.
In them we have an example:
   for the strengthening of our faith,
   for the quality of Christian life,
   for the joyousness of the life-style.
We—the saints of this age—recall them,
the saints of ages gone by
that we might be drawn to Christ,
to his freeing power in Resurection,
as were the Fathers of the Revolution.
We join them in the one catholic faith,
share with them the hope of new humanity,
celebrate with them the love and peace of God.
Living or dead, we are the community of faith,
called by the Spirit into new life.

MORE SONGS

THE OFFERING PERIOD

THE EXTENSION OF THE COMMUNITY
   1. announcement of any coming events
   2. statement of purpose for the next celebration
   3. introduction of newcomers to the community

SONG BEFORE THE COMMUNION LITURGY *(optional)*

FATHERS OF THE REVOLUTION
   THE RECONCILIATION PERIOD *(Face-to-face discussion, etc.)*

   THE KISS OF PEACE
      V. Salute your brothers and sisters with a kiss.
      R. We celebrate the community of the revolution.

   THE SONG BEFORE THE MEAL *(optional)*

   THE THANKSGIVING PRAYER
Before you we stand like beggars before the king, knowing the
long history of beggars and clowns, thinkers and actors, in which
we stand. We give thanks for these lives gone before us, our mod-

els for the faith: for the women who knew in Christ the gentleness and power of all mankind, Mary, Mary Magdalene, Salome and others; for gentle Francis of Assisi and Martin Luther King, for all the spiritual fathers—the *startsi* of Russia, for the pilgrims like John XXIII and A. J. Muste, who strove for peace and unity; for the holy men of the red nations—visionaries like Black Elk and Wovoka; for the lyric poets who sang of life—Milton and Chaucer and others; for George Fox and William Penn and John Woolman and Elizabeth Fry, peaceful people of action of the Quaker faith; for the activists—S. John Chrysostom, Thomas Muenzer, Dietrich Bonhoeffer, and others; for all who outlined the community-nature of the faith, especially Basil of Caesarea, Christoph Blumhardt, and Thomas Merton; for visionaries like Teresa of Avila, Catherine of Siena, Ursula, Dorothy Day, and Dorothy Hutchinson; for all the saints of history and for all the saints who gather here at this time, we give thanks. We affirm them as men and women by whom we are assisted to find ourselves. We stand in line of this great community from whom there is much to be learned and through whom we gain strength.

But especially do we give thanks for him in whom all the community began, our brother Jesus of Nazareth, who in the night of his betrayal took bread and gave thanks and broke it and gave it to his friend, saying, "Take and eat: this is my body given for you." Likewise, he took the cup of wine after he had drunk from it, gave thanks and gave it them, saying, "Drink of this, all of you: it is my blood, which creates the new human society." We do this in memory of him.

Spirit of power, be with us to empower our lives for faith and service and love. Enable us through the sign of our faith in this meal to grow in love and understanding toward one another and the world. Show us the Truth which has set men free and is freeing us even now. Amen.

THE OUR FATHER

V. As often as we eat this bread and drink this cup:
R. We show forth the Lord's death until he comes.
V. Celebrate the history of the revolution.
R. The revolution continues in our minds and hearts!

THE MEAL

THE CLOSING THANKSGIVING PRAYER

CLOSING SONGS

THE BLESSINGS

V. Shall we thank the Lord once more?

R. Yes, we'll thank him once again.

V. Bless we the Lord.

R. Thanks be to God, who gave the revolution.

V. Go forth into the world with love.

Celebrate the revolution of peace and freedom.

Remember your fathers, who carved the community.

Build the community wherever and whenever you can.

In the name and for the sake of Christ.

R. So be it. So shall we live!

9

DRAMATIC PRESENTATION
IN THE LITURGY

The revolutionary year is a dramatic presentation of the Christian reality-model by way of the rehearsal of specific points in
time each year for and with the people of God. It retains an identity as a way for God to move to man in grace. The liturgical
celebration may be, to some extent, manipulable, but it is not
possible to ignore its basis in the concept of God's coming to man
without destroying its integrity and turning it into sloppy moral-
ism, a "service of edification." The liturgy is not meant to be
man's thoughts about God so much as it is God's action toward
man.

The revolutionary year is a means by which the church im-
merses people in the historical consciousness of what it means to
be Christian. The Saints' Days, as Luther maintained, should be
celebrated because they are an occasion for seeing how faith
was lived in other eras, an occasion for the strengthening of one's
own faith. We live in a historical milieu; the church year serves
to sensitize us to the Christian interpretation of that milieu. To
do this, it rehearses the great festivals of the life of Christ: birth,
manifestation to the world, ministry, passion, death and resurrection, ascension and Pentecost (which is a festival of Christ, really,
since the liturgical texts leading up to it remind us that it is on

the basis of Christ's promise that the Spirit—the Paraclete—comes to us). Over one-half of the revolutionary year is Christ's; the other half is the church's. The revolutionary year is a conscious effort to draw out the implications of the Christ-event for the life of the community. In a way, the parallel to the church year within the Bible would be Paul's letter to the Romans, which rehearses the meaning of Christ for eleven chapters, concluding with a hymn of praise, then moves into the ethical ramifications in Chapter 12 with what someone has called the "great 'therefore'." Romans is a revolutionary book; the church's year of grace is a revolutionary year.

The church year is cultus; it is composed of ritual acts, no matter how stripped down they may become in a house-church liturgy. We do not live without cultus, any more than we live without myth. Not only is man a mythopoeic creature, he also produces cultus to celebrate his myths. Left-wing Protestantism lost a lot when it abandoned the cultus of the catholic church. Those of us in church traditions which retained the cultus have a lot of material to work with to give new meaning to symbol and sign.

The function of this chapter is to offer some directions for a liturgical house-church celebration which will retain a sense of mystery and drama. We see basically three components to this celebration: first, there is *drama* itself; second, there is *proclamation*; and third, there is the *environment* in which celebration takes place (this includes the behavioral style of the liturgical president, which is highly important for house-church liturgical celebrations).

The *drama* of the liturgy is rather obvious. The gospel may be many things to many people, indeed it has to be to be the gospel, but at its root it is a story. Paul speaks in Galatians of "placarding the gospel before men," of telling the story that is the gospel. This story has two halves: the *origin* of the gospel (the "story" of Christ) and the *outreach* of the gospel (the "story" of the church). The two halves of the story are rehearsed during the church year. The function of the traditional propers in a liturgical system of dramatization is to shift the emphasis from week to week so that the total story is told and people don't get hung up on one chapter. The liturgical system has its faults, but it safeguards the people of God from clergy who feel called to pluck one note on the harp of the gospel year in and year out. Followed consciously, the liturgical system has a well-rounded shape, despite its age and the antiquity of many of its words. In contemporary worship, it is possible to strip down the liturgical system and yet retain the perspective and the shape of the year; that is what the seasonal celebrations in this book are all about.

Part of the drama comes through also in the "staging" of the year, to follow the analogy of a drama. The staging in the catholic tradition consists of the additional symbols used during the year, e.g., ashes for Ash Wednesday, palms for Palm Sunday, and the like. The things of the earth are used in conscious celebration of the earth as God's creation and gift to man. Beyond this, of course, there is the historic tie which many of the old traditions provide; they set the stage for a contemporary understanding of the ancient story. That is all they do however, and we lose the battle at the beginning if we don't realize that their link with the present is not apparent to all the people. The task of the liturgical president as dramatist must be to show the links between ancient symbol and present reality. Apart from this, the liturgy remains a mystery in the wrong sense of the word, and people walk away from it thinking, "it was a good show, but it didn't really touch me personally." As people see *themselves* in the story that is told through the drama of the liturgy, however, they are assisted in developing that inner consciousness of the history of their faith which enables them to live it in a contemporary world.

The drama is enhanced by periods of silence. Too much crowds and vies for attention in much church worship; time is not provided for reflection on what's happening; consequently, people's heads are crammed full of information and representations that they never have the time to think about. There is an information overload in a lot of the catholic liturgy; time must be given to sort it through. Out of this sorting frequently comes new insight which can be shared with the whole group; this is our way of building the "Quaker mode" into worship. Often the silence is not broken, because a mystery of Christ has so profoundly touched the participants that there is nothing to do but reflect on it until a later time when it will be possible to speak about it.

The *proclamation* in the liturgy is not limited to preaching. All liturgical patterns, if they have been thought out, contain a proclamation. The little liturgies in this book are shaped with several proclamatory devices. Among these devices, there is first of all the retention of the skeleton of the historic liturgy itself (liturgy of the word, affirmation, offering, reconciliation and kiss of peace, prayer, liturgy of the Sacrament, dismissal into the world). Beyond this, there is the proclamatory use of the biblical texts for the theme of worship, and the use of a Psalm for antiphonal reading. There are also seasonal affirmations and eucharistic prayers. Each liturgy retains the same basic pattern but shifts the emphasis slightly and offers a slight explanation of the meaning of each season of the revolutionary year. There is a balance between emotion and intellect, between individual input and declaration of God's grace, in these liturgies when they are celebrated. They need to be handled with joy more than grim solemnity.

The words of the celebration ought to penetrate to the level of *meaning*. We cannot be satisfied with words that are traditional and ancient, if they no longer bear a meaning from within the context of experience.

The liturgy is primarily doxological and eucharistic. (It may also be didactic, in that stripped to its skeleton it offers a demonstration model for the Christian life-style). Its function is to praise and offer thanks to God, whom we have seen in the reality and meaning of our own personal experience and in the great historic events of the faith. Thanks and praise are only relevant when the sacred dimension of life is recognized by the individual. Hence, praise rests on individual religious experience. In the liturgy we have a framework through which to offer praise. It is not perfect and never will be, because it is impossible to create a style that offers meaning to everyone at all times. The liturgy is meant to take the feelings and the thoughts of the people and to offer them. A sermon fits this doxological structure, too; it is not to be primarily didactic, because if it is it will avert the consciousness of the participant from contemplation to rational speculation. Within the liturgical structure, a sermon which calls for a great deal of intellectual work detracts from the remainder of the liturgy. The sermon is a means of celebrating the mystery of God's presence in life; it is not a historical recital of doctrines. The pulpit is not the place to test out intellectual theories; it is the place to celebrate verbally the presence of God within humanity. The Eucharist is a parable, a fantasy of life within the kingdom of God, a life marked by the unification of mankind within the reality of God. When this is obscured, the Eucharist becomes a mere act unconnected to all of life. The sacramental principle is a universal; it is focused in certain actions of the church only so as to lead people to see the interrelationship of God and world in *all* areas of life. Our doxology emphasizes this; the sermon should emphasize it; the Eucharist's relationships to all of life must continually be explored.

The liturgy performs the function of opening up consciousness to the presence of God. It is a consciousness-raising device; its continuing usefulness is in offering "hooks" for the definition of religious experience. The process is aborted when the religious experience of the individual is not affirmed (as it is not in much Protestant worship), when the intimations of the divine which people sense in their lives are shoved aside to make room for the historic recital of the faith. What we must seek is balance—balance between emphasizing personal religious experience to the exclusion of the historic proclamation of the faith and emphasizing the historic reality to the exclusion of contemporary experience. Between these two extremes lies a middle ground wherein the catholic liturgy can have its place and work its benefits for the lives of individuals and communities. Experience separated from the historic reality winds up a solipsistic subjectivism; we might wish this were not the case, but unfortunately it is. On the other hand, the presentation of objective reality without clear, demonstrable links to the life of man winds up barren and arid. The balance lies between these two extremes . . . as it always has.

The behavioral model of the liturgical president becomes crucial when we take the foregoing into consideration. The liturgical president cannot dictate religious experience; he must allow it free expression, encourage it, not criticize it so that growth is aborted. To this end, silence is a good introduction into even the traditional liturgy; there is more than enough time for words. More time ought to be allowed for silent contemplation. The liturgical president must set a standard of openness and awareness, must open himself to the interpretation of his *own* experience, must allow himself to be surprised by God's presence, must reopen the doors to serendipity and wonder. The liturgical president should be less concerned about filling a void with his own erudition and more concerned with sharing himself in the name of God. Other times are preferable for straight teaching than the context of a celebration. He must be convinced that the signs of God's presence include joy, laughter, spontaneous displays of affection, and a sort of playful approach to life which does not set itself grim-faced against the world. Preeminently he will remember and rejoice that theology is poetic and liturgy is essentially a dance to the music of life. He will understand that the world is an act of play on the part of God and that suffering cannot be taken too seriously because the base of reality is love. Yet he will paradoxically understand the suffering of the world as a negative insight into the meaning of God, and seek to dethrone the "gods" of this world in system and institution.

The liturgical president must take seriously his altered role in the celebrations given in this book. He is the *manager* of the liturgical process and no longer its *proprietor*. He will be willing to share the functions of the liturgy, viewing himself as master of ceremonies rather than ceremonial master. Everything in the liturgy can be shared; the president retains a form of order in the process and understands himself as participating (primarily) through sermon and eucharistic prayer. These are his functions; as part of the people, this is his work. But others have their work, too. Total participation is not only encouraged, it is essential in small-group worship. Without it, nothing happens. It may take a period of growth for this to begin to happen fully, but it is an aim in small-group worship, and the liturgical president must set an open environment by his behavior for this kind of total participation.

10

THE PLACE OF CELEBRATION
IN CHRISTIANITY

One of the continuing experiences that we have had in using the small-group approach to worship along the lines of a reunderstood liturgical year has been the realization that the celebration-life is really very *central* to a Christian life-style. It is not at all peripheral. Those who celebrate with us are convinced of the centrality of the liturgical celebrations. In many cases (since we work with students, many of whom return home in the summer), the feedback has indicated that participation in the celebration-life of the Community of the Spirit has prepared them for understanding the traditional liturgical patterns in their home churches during the summer months. But the point is the *centrality* of the celebration-life.

The church of the East has long recognized the mystical nature of Christian liturgy. Western Christianity seems to have made two errors with regard to the liturgy. On one hand, it has emphasized the didactic function of the liturgy and minimized its doxological/mystical nature. On the other hand, it has aborted participation by putting the responsibility for the worship life in the hands of the few. As a result of these errors a gulf has been growing between the liturgy and the people over the years, so that it is dreadfully difficult for most people even to give the liturgical pattern a chance to put back some of the mystery that is lacking in their lives. In large measure, the search for the renewal of mystery is one of the basic reasons for the house-church and experimental-liturgy route many are now taking.

Small-group celebrations exhibit three characteristics which we have noted at various places throughout this book, but which it may be helpful to note in sequence now. These three characteristics are: (1) it is a model for the Christian life-style; (2) it is a framework for organizing religious experience into a meaningful whole; and (3) it is a medium through which God's love may be experienced in and through others.

The celebration offers a small-scale demonstration of what life within a functioning Christian community looks like. In some ways, this is not due to the celebration but rather to the ongoing system of relationships which make up the Christian community. But part of it is due to the celebration pattern itself. Among the things that are mirrored for all to see and reflect upon in the celebration are the use of the word as a framework for life and reflection, the openness to one another that is shown in both the reconciliation period and kiss of peace, the sharing of a common meal and a common vision of the future in the Eucharist, the focus on the "virtues" of peace, joy, love, hope, and faith. These are components of the Christian life-style which are modeled in the celebration of the community. In this respect primarily, the celebration is a teaching tool for today.

This whole book has been dedicated to showing that the celebration is a way of organizing religious experience throughout the seasons of the revolutionary year. No further note is really needed to clarify or add to this idea. Suffice it to say that all of individual religious experience can find a home within one part of the revolutionary year seasons. This is a broad statement and it is capable of instant criticism; but examine the church's year and its liturgical pattern carefully. It leaves no meaningful religious experience outside its net.

Lastly, the celebration offers a medium through which God's love may be experienced in and through others. It partakes of the character of a "means of grace," because the means of grace (in traditional definition) are to be found within its scope: baptism, the Eucharist, absolution, and the "sacrament of the word" itself. This is a hard saying for modern man. I ponder it even as I write it down. Who can understand these things, that in bread and wine and in water and word there is an expression of divine love conveyed to man which is objectively true, apart from our perception of it? We live in an age in which the great hang-up of religious seekers is their demand for subjective experience. We have tried to say in this book that subjective experience is matched by objective reality in Christianity. But the validation is from the objective to the subjective, and not the other way around. This is the central faith of Christianity and it cannot be turned round without losing the objectivity and wonder-fullness of grace. There are many within the Christian faith whose view of God's love is so "supernatural" that it never connects with the ordinary events of life; yet this is what the sacramental principle is all about. We celebrate the infusion of a part of life with the divine as a symbol that all of life is now infused with the divine through the Incarnation. But the Incarnation proves the infusion, and not vice versa; otherwise we are reduced to subjective experience again and the hope for absolute truth evades us. Christianity holds that absolute truth is focused in the mystery of the Resurrection of Christ. All celebration is related to this one mystery; all of the sacramental life is related to it, too, as the hub around which the spokes of the wheel radiate.

Celebration, with its three characteristics, is thus *logically* very central in Christianity. It is the means through which community is created and sustained. The church has no other means, really, by which to build community than the liturgical patterns; that is their function.

At the same time, it ought to be said that celebration is for the *committed*. In contrast with what has come to be associated with Sunday worship patterns in Protestant churches, celebration is an alternative which is demanding of the participant. Demanding in terms of personal commitment to the liturgical process; demanding in terms of personal input in the celebration itself; demanding in terms of personal behavior within the liturgical celebration. In small-group worship, no matter how it is structured, there is a demand put on the participants. In the celebration-pattern, there is even more of a demand. This is more than a meeting for worship; it is a demonstration of how life can operate (even if only on a small scale and for a short time-period) within the Christian life-style on a communal level. This makes it demanding.

Our experience with this form of worship has taught us that there is another side to the whole question of liturgical renewal. If it be true (so goes the common assumption) that most Sunday worship is too dry, too uninteresting, for people to get into it, then there is another side to the whole matter: we believe the celebration-pattern is too *real* for some people to get involved with. For this reason, we would never suggest it as the basic worship life for most congregations. Christian communities can profitably use it and gain thereby. It is, however, not suited to the needs of a large congregation and cannot be used for regular Sunday worship there. It is meant for those who are *committed* to the Christian life-style, and it is meant for those who see the *centrality* of worship for their lives. Working from a base of people who fill the bill as far as these criteria are concerned, the celebration-pattern then moves on to incorporate and train new people in commitment and the centrality of celebration.

FOR FURTHER READING

FOR FURTHER READING

(See also the resources listed in *Create and Celebrate*)

A. PREACHING

Bartlett, Gene. *The Audacity of Preaching.* New York: Harper & Row, 1962.

Bass, George. *The Renewal of Liturgical Preaching.* Minneapolis: Augsburg Publishing House, 1967.

Buttrick, George A. *Jesus Came Preaching.* Grand Rapids, Mich.: Baker Book House, 1970.

Caemmerer, Richard R. *Preaching for the Church.* St. Louis: Concordia Publishing House, 1959.

Davis, H. Grady. *Design for Preaching.* Philadelphia: Fortress Press, 1958.

Farmer, H. H. *The Servant of the Word.* Edited by Gilbert E. Doan. Philadelphia: Fortress Press, 1964.

Forsyth, P. T. *Positive Preaching and the Modern Mind.* Grand Rapids, Mich.: Eerdmans Publishing Co., 1964.

Hunter, Archibald. *Teaching and Preacing the New Testament.* Philadelphia: Westminster Press, 1963.

Ritschl, Dietrich. *The Theology of Proclamation.* Richmond, Va.: John Knox Press, 1960.

Wingren, Gustav. *The Living Word.* Philadelphia: Fortress Press, 1965.

B. LITURGY: THE YEAR

Herrlin, Olof. *The Divine Service: Liturgy in Perspective.* Philadelphia: Fortress Press, 1966.

Horn, Edward T. *The Christian Year.* Philadelphia: Fortress Press, 1957.

111

Lindemann, Fred. *Sermon and the Propers.* Four volumes. St. Louis: Concordia Publishing House, 1958.

Parsch, Pius. *The Church's Year of Grace.* Five volumes. Collegeville, Minn., 1953.

Shepherd, Massey. *The Worship of the Church.* New York: Seabury Press, 1952.

C. THEOLOGY

Cox, Harvey. *The Feast of Fools.* Cambridge, Mass.: Harvard University Press, 1969.

Keen, Sam. *Apology for Wonder.* New York: Harper & Row, 1969.

_____. *To a Dancing God.* New York: Harper & Row, 1970.

Künneth, Walter. *Theology of the Resurrrection.* St. Louis: Concordia Publishing House, 1965.

Schmemann, Alexander. *Ultimate Questions.* New York: Holt, Rinehart & Winston, 1965.

D. GENERAL

Bloy, Myron. *Multi-media Worship.* New York: Seabury Press, 1969.

Frankl, Viktor. *Man's Search for Meaning.* Boston: Beacon Press, 1963.

Illich, Ivan. *Celebration of Awareness.* New York: Doubleday and Co., 1971.

Toffler, Alvin. *Future Shock.* New York: Random House, 1970.